ANCIENT REMEDIES REVIVED BOOK

500+ Herbal & Natural Remedies (Traditional Healing
Secrets for the Modern Age)

BY
ANICOL WARFEZ

Table of Content

INTRODUCTION

Ancient Remedies Revived takes the reader on a trip through the history of time to show the rich history of plant medicine, which goes back as far as people can remember. This research isn't just for fun; it's a call to find and use our ancestors' knowledge in our current lives to improve our health and well-being. Ancient Mesopotamia's rich gardens and India and China's holy books both talk about how plants can heal. This is a theme that runs through all of human history. The way we see and use medical plants today is shaped by the knowledge and practices of many different civilizations, each with its unique view of the natural world. Together, the ancient and modern worlds are brought in this book to show that the secrets of the past can help us solve today health problems today's health problems. We find the basic ideas behind plant medicine by carefully looking at old books, artefacts from archaeology, and traditional ways of doing things. These rules are not old wives' tales; they are modern pieces of knowledge that can solve health problems in the 21st century. We want people of all ages and walks of life to join us on this trip as we look into the history and development of herbalism. This book is helpful for anyone interested in the art and science of herbal medicine, no matter how experienced they are or how new they are to the world of healing plants. We want to help people feel more connected to nature and give them the tools they need to use plants' healing power by giving them both historical background and helpful advice. Join us as we restore old treatments, exploring how they can be integrated into modern life to promote health, boost immunity, ease stress, and improve well-being. This is not just a book about plants; it is a trip into the heart of healing, a celebration of the ancient knowledge that ties us to the earth and each other.

GLOBAL MEDICINAL HERBS: CULTURAL ORIGINS

The use of medical plants runs across various countries, each with unique practices and ideas that have significantly added to the base of herbal medicine as we understand it today. These old practices offer a view into how our ancestors dealt with the natural world, utilizing the plants around them for healing, holy purposes, and daily health care. In ancient Mesopotamia, one of the oldest cradles of culture, medicine plants were catalogued on clay plates, showing extensive pharmacopoeia. The Sumerians, for instance, described the use of plants such as Thyme and liquorice for their healing powers. This careful recording of herbal knowledge underscores the importance of plants in Mesopotamian society, not only for their healing value but also for their role in holy rites. Moving to the banks of the Nile, ancient Egyptians harnessed the power of herbs in healing and burying methods. Papyrus papers, such as the Ebers Papyrus, record the use of over 850 plant-based medicines, showing ancient Egyptian doctors' vast herbal knowledge. Aloe vera was frequently used for its healing and soothing properties, while Garlic was valued for its health-promoting effects. The rich weave of plant medicine also runs to old India, where the practice of Ayurveda, a complete healing method, has grown for thousands of years. Ayurveda supports the balance between body, mind, and spirit, including medicine, herbs, food, and lifestyle changes. Ashwagandha, for instance, is praised for its adaptogenic qualities, helping the body fight stresses, while Tulsi or Holy Basil is respected for its spiritual and medical importance. In ancient China, the creation of Traditional Chinese Medicine (TCM) brought a complicated system of study and treatment, mixing plants into a framework that tries to balance the body's natural energy, or Qi. The Chinese Materia Medica, a medical reference book, lists thousands of medicine substances, including plants like Ginseng, known for its energy-boosting traits, and Ginkgo Biloba, used to improve brain function. The ancient Greeks also significantly improved herbal medicine, with figures like Hippocrates and Dioscorides laying the groundwork for modern herbalism. Hippocrates, often called the father of medicine, pushed for using food and plants to avoid and treat illness. Dioscorides' De Materia Medica, an entire book on plant medicine, stayed an essential guide for over a thousand years. As these societies interacted with their surroundings, they deeply understood the plants around them, leading to various herbal practices worldwide. This world custom of plant medicine is not just a testament to human creativity and adaptability; it also gives valuable insights into sustainable health practices supporting modern medicine. By learning these old practices, we respect our elders and better understand the natural world and its ability to heal and help.

HERBAL MEDICINE THROUGH THE AGES

The historical growth of plant medicine is an exciting trip that shows the adaptability and cleverness of human cultures in their drive for health and well-being. From the old world to today, using plants for medical reasons has experienced significant shifts shaped by discoveries, cultural trades, and scientific improvements. This growth is not merely a record of changed practices but a testament to the continuing trust in the healing power of nature. In the old world, plant treatment was deeply linked with life's spiritual and valuable parts. The Egyptians, for instance, were pioneers in collecting plant knowledge and making some of the oldest known medical records. Their understanding of flowers was practical for healing diseases and symbolic of the funeral process.

Similarly, in ancient Greece, the works of Hippocrates set the basis for plant medicine by stressing the worth of food and natural health, an idea that would echo through the ages. The Roman Empire furthered the spread of plant knowledge, with doctors like Galen building upon Greek practices and making huge books that would rule European medicine for ages. The fall of the Roman Empire saw a change towards the monks keeping and growing plant knowledge. Monastic gardens became places of medical plant growth, and monks mixed local folk customs with traditional knowledge, playing a crucial part in the survival and spread of herbal medicine during the Middle Ages. The Renaissance marked a significant turning point, defined by a return of interest in old works and a growing spirit of inquiry. The printing press helped spread herbal knowledge, with herbals—comprehensive books on plants and their uses—becoming highly popular. This age also saw the beginning of more organized ways of studying plants, setting the groundwork for modern biology. The Age of Exploration in the 15th and 16th centuries gave Europeans a wealth of new plants from the Americas, Africa, and Asia, significantly growing the materia medica available to herbalists. This time of cross-cultural contact brought about a profound shift in plant medicine as new methods were introduced into European practices. However, the rise of modern science in the 17th and 18th centuries weakened plant habits. The development of chemistry and the focus on single, active ingredients led to a drop in the use of whole plants and a growing split between traditional herbalism and the new field of standard medicine. Despite this, plant care continued to grow among indigenous peoples and in rural places, where traditional knowledge was passed down through generations. The 19th and early 20th centuries saw an increased interest in plant medicine, merging with the Romantic movement's focus on nature and industry critique. This time, they witnessed the birth of herbalism as an official job in some parts of the world, with schools and groups dedicated to the study and practice of herbal treatment. In recent decades, there has been a rise in interest in plant medicine, driven by more scientific studies proving the usefulness of many traditional treatments and a broad desire for more natural and organic health methods. Today, plant care is at an intersection where old knowledge meets new science. It is increasingly blended into the standard healthcare system, with many traditional practitioners knowing the worth of plant drugs as complementary treatments. The growth of plant medicine is an echo of humanity's continued desire for health and well-being. It is a story of adaptation and endurance; knowledge passed down through the ages, and the ongoing balance between custom and creativity. As we look to the future, the lessons of the past tell us of the importance of saving this rich history while improving the science of plant medicine for the benefit of all.

The rise of interest in herbal medicine indicates a more significant change towards organic and preventive health care, where the worth of natural treatments, including herbs, is generally accepted in modern medicine. This acceptance is not merely a custom return but is backed by a more significant amount of scientific study backing plant medicines' usefulness and possible benefits. Today, herbs are essential in complementary and alternative medicine (CAM), giving a natural, friendly, and often cost-effective approach to health and fitness. In modern medicine, herbs are utilized in various ways, including drinks, drugs, pills, and topicals, to treat different conditions. Their application spans from improving general well-being and immune function to handling specific health problems such as gut disorders, worry, anxiety, and chronic diseases. The integration of herbal medicine into modern healthcare practices is facilitated by practitioners of both conventional and alternative medicine who recognize the potential of herbs to complement traditional treatments and, in some cases, offer a preferable alternative to pharmaceuticals due to their lower incidence of side effects. One of the key reasons driving the current importance of herbs in medicine is the general attitude they mirror. Unlike conventional drugs that often target particular symptoms or systems, herbs can provide multiple benefits, working closely with the body's natural processes to restore balance and health. This holistic viewpoint is beautiful in treating chronic diseases and in preventive health care, where the goal is to support the general functioning of the body rather than simply treating individual symptoms.

Furthermore, the current pharmaceutical business has its roots in herbal medicine, with many drugs being taken from chemicals found in plants. Studying traditional plant medicines continues to inspire pharmaceutical research, making new drugs that harness the active chemicals in herbs. This ongoing conversation between traditional herbalism and modern pharmacology shows the importance of herbs in current medicine, showing their promise as a source of new healing agents. The growing customer interest in natural and organic items has also led to the greater use of herbs in health and fitness. This trend is backed by a desire for more open and sustainable healthcare choices, with people looking to take a more active part in controlling their health using natural treatments. The abundance of herbal items has grown dramatically, with herbs now widely available in health food stores, hospitals, and online, making it easier for people to adopt herbal medicine into their healthcare practice. Despite the growing acceptance of herbs in modern medicine, challenges remain, including the need for more thorough scientific studies to show the usefulness and safety of herbal drugs and the importance of teaching practitioners and customers about the proper use of plants. The quality and standards of herbal items are also significant problems, with variety in the strength and purity of herbal medicines affecting their safety and effectiveness.

In conclusion, the role of herbs in current health is varied and growing. As we continue to study the links between old knowledge and modern science, herbs offer positive answers for better health and well-being. Their addition to modern health care methods shows a bigger view of health that values natural, integrative techniques alongside standard medicine. As study improves and knowledge grows, the ability of plant medicine to add to modern health care will likely continue to change, giving new options for healing and wellness.

FUNDAMENTAL PRINCIPLES OF HERBAL MEDICINE

Herbal medicine, an old art based on the very structure of human history, works on a set of core principles that separate it from standard medicine. These ideas are not merely rules but are the core of how herbalists view health, sickness, and the restoring process. At the heart of plant medicine lies the trust in the healing power of nature, an idea known as vis medicatrix naturae. This theory suggests that the body can fix itself and that medicine plants support this natural healing process. Unlike conventional drugs that often target particular symptoms, plant medicine tries to address the root cause of an illness, looking for a complete fix of balance within the body. One of the basic tenets of herbal medicine is the idea of balance, where the whole plant is thought to be more effective than its different parts. This general way varies from the reductionist standpoint of modern medicine, which often focuses on single, active chemicals.

Herbalists say that the complicated interaction of chemicals within a plant adds to its positive effect, lowering the risk of side effects and promoting a more balanced mending process. Another key idea is the value of individualization in care. Herbal medicine knows that each person is unique, with their own genetic, environmental, and social factors affecting their health. Consequently, plant drugs are modified to the person, taking into account not only their symptoms but also their general attitude and the underlying problems adding to their condition. This personalized method ensures the treatment handles the patient's unique needs, promoting more effective and lasting healing. Protection is also core to plant medicine, stressing the value of staying healthy and avoiding disease before it happens. This protective method is reflected in tonic herbs that boost the body's processes, raise health, and improve stress tolerance. By supporting the body's natural defences, plant medicine avoids sickness, lowers the chance of chronic disease, and promotes general well-being.

Additionally, plant medicine strongly focuses on the healing link between the practitioner and the patient. This link is marked by mutual respect, teamwork, and a deep understanding of the patient's experience of sickness. The herbalist's job is to propose plant drugs and teach and inspire the patient, supporting active participation in their mending process. Sustainability and ethical sources of healing plants are also vital in herbal medicine. With the growing demand for herbal drugs, there is a rising need to ensure that plants are collected carefully without lowering local populations or hurting the environment. Herbalists fight for sustainable practices, such as organic farming and responsible wildcrafting, to keep the purity of medicine plants and the surroundings from which they are taken. Following these ideas includes a full patient review, including their medical background, habits, and mental well-being. The healer then picks suitable herbs to build a unique treatment plan, considering their traits, actions, and energetics. This plan may include different plant products, such as drinks, potions, pills, or topicals, to support the body's mending process and restore balance. Blending these basic principles into plant medicine shows a deep respect for the knowledge of nature and the complexity of the human body. By taking a complete, focused, and preventive approach to health, plant medicine offers a robust and permanent path to well-being based on the timeless knowledge of old practices and improved by the insights of modern science.

MECHANISMS OF MEDICINAL HERBS

Medicinal herbs work through a complicated chemical mix that fully interacts with the body's internal processes. Unlike drugs that generally target specific spots or receptors in the body, the ingredients of medicine plants can perform multiple actions due to their wide range of valuable chemicals. This complex way helps herbs treat not just the signs but the root reasons of health problems, encouraging balance and repair in the body. The main methods herbs produce their effects include phytochemical actions on the body's molecular processes and organ systems. Phytochemicals are naturally formed substances in plants that have safe, disease-preventing compounds. These include alkaloids, flavonoids, glycosides, and terpenes, each with unique therapeutic traits. Alkaloids, for example, have a marked effect on the nervous system and can change mood and pain perception. Flavonoids are known for their antioxidant and anti-inflammatory traits, helping to protect the body against oxidative stress and inflammation.

Herbs also work by controlling the defence system. Certain herbs can improve immune function, making the body more effective at beating infections and diseases. Echinacea and astragalus, for instance, boost the immune system, boosting the activity of white blood cells and other components of the immune responses. Different plants, such as liquorice root, can control the immune system, lowering excessive immune reactions in conditions like allergies and autoimmune diseases. Another major way herbs work is by regulating the endocrine system, which controls hormones. Herbs such as ashwagandha and holy basil can help handle the body's stress response by controlling the production of stress hormones like cortisol. This not only helps in handling stress and worry but also improves general adrenal health. Herbs also affect the digestive system, helping in processing, easing pain, and supporting gut health. Bitter plants like dandelion and gentian support stomach juices and improve the breakdown and uptake of nutrients. Herbs with high fibre content, such as psyllium, support gut function and can ease constipation.

Detoxification is another critical mode of action for many herbs. They support the body's natural cleaning processes, helping to remove poisons from the body. Milk thistle, for example, is famous for its liver-protective effects, improving liver function and boosting the regrowth of liver cells. The artery system also gets from the action of medicine herbs. Hawthorn, Garlic, and Ginger are known to improve heart health by changing blood pressure, cholesterol levels, and circulation. These herbs can help treat and control circulation diseases by boosting the heart and blood vessels and improving blood flow. On a molecular level, many herbs show anti-cancer traits by causing apoptosis (programmed cell death) in cancer cells, stopping tumour growth, and protecting against DNA damage. Turmeric, whose main ingredient is curcumin, is widely studied for its anti-inflammatory and anti-cancer effects, showing hope in cancer prevention and treatment. It is vital to understand that the value of medicinal herbs is affected by various factors, including the quality of the herb, the way of preparation, and the individual's unique body state. The inclusive nature of herbal medicine means that the same herb can affect different people differently, underlining the value of individual care.

In summary, medicine plants work through several processes, working with the body's systems fully and perfectly. Their ability to influence multiple paths simultaneously is what sets them apart from conventional drugs, giving them a complete approach to health and healing. Understanding how herbs work is essential to reaching their full medical potential, allowing people to integrate herbal medicine into their health plans successfully.

CHEMICAL COMPONENTS AND EFFECTS OF HERBS

The active factors in herbs, basically their chemical components, are the source of their healing benefits. These components interact with the human body complexly, changing internal processes and adding to the herbs' healing powers. Understanding these active principles is essential for achieving the full promise of plant medicine. Alkaloids, one of the main active components found in plants, are nitrogen-containing molecules known for their powerful medical benefits. They can have different effects, including painkiller (pain-relieving), antispasmodic (relieving cramps), and antibiotic properties. For example, morphine, a drug found in the poppy flower, is a strong painkiller, while quinine from the bark of the Cinchona tree is antimalarial. Flavonoids are another critical group of chemicals generally known for their antioxidant and anti-inflammatory benefits. These chemicals help remove dangerous free radicals in the body, lower reaction stress, and avoid cell damage. The anti-inflammatory action of flavonoids makes them helpful in treating illnesses like gout and heart disease. Herbs rich in flavonoids include chamomile, known for its calming and anti-inflammatory benefits, and hawthorn, used in treating heart-related problems. Glycosides, chemicals that give one or more sugars upon breakdown, have different effects on the human body, including heart function and immune system management. Cardiac glycosides, for example, found in herbs like foxglove (Digitalis purpurea), are used for their heart-strengthening and arrhythmia-correcting properties. Saponins, another type of glycoside, have immune-modulating and expectorant actions, making them helpful in treating colds and boosting the immune system. Terpenes and terpenoids, the most significant class of natural goods, are known for their pleasant traits and are the main parts of essential oils. Beyond their lovely smell, terpenes have been shown to contain anti-inflammatory, antibacterial, and healing properties. For instance, menthol from peppermint provides a cooling feeling and lowers pain, while limonene from citrus peels has anti-inflammatory and antioxidant benefits.

Tannins are polyphenolic chemicals that have calming qualities, which can help in wound healing and lowering inflammation. They are found in different plants, including witch hazel, used for its skin-soothing benefits.

Combining these chemical components with the body's biological processes underscores the general nature of plant medicine. Unlike produced medicines that often target a particular spot or receptor, the active principles in plants can perform a wide range of effects, addressing not only the symptoms but also the root causes of health problems. This open way supports balance and healing in the body, meeting natural health goals.

Moreover, the balance between different components within a single plant or among different herbs in a mixture can improve medical benefits and reduce the risk of side effects. This synergistic interaction, where the total effect is greater than the sum of individual effects, is a crucial feature of the success of plant treatment. Studying and understanding the active principles of herbs are essential for both practitioners and users of herbal medicine. It allows the picking of acceptable herbs and recipes matched to individual needs, improving the healing potential of herbal medicine. As the study continues to find the processes by which these chemical components perform their effects, the merging of plant medicine into natural health practices will likely grow, giving a complementary and sustainable approach to health and wellness.

HERBAL VS. CONVENTIONAL MEDICINE: A COMPARISON

Herbal and traditional medicine represent two different ways of mending, each with its skills, beliefs, and effects. The comparison between these two types of medicine is not just about success but also includes their approach to disease, treatment methods, patient involvement, and side effects, among other factors. At the heart of plant medicine lies a holistic approach that sees the body as a related system. This viewpoint stresses the value of helping the whole person rather than separating symptoms or diseases. Herbalists often take into account a patient's lifestyle, food, and mental well-being alongside their physical problems. This complete method aims to restore balance and unity within the body, leveraging the body's natural ability to fix itself. Medicinal herbs are used for their varied effects on the body, often treating multiple problems simultaneously due to their complex phytochemical makeup.

The practice of plant medicine is firmly based on traditional knowledge and the practical results of generations, though current science studies increasingly back it. Conversely, standard medicine is marked by a reductionist approach that focuses on specific diseases or symptoms, often through the lens of the latest science and technology breakthroughs. It relies heavily on drugs and surgery to treat health problems, with meds meant to target specific body processes or bacteria. These drugs are based on thorough scientific studies, including randomized controlled studies, to show efficiency and safety. Conventional medicine shines in acute care and cases where fast action is necessary, such as surgery, emergency care, and life-threatening diseases. One of the critical differences between herbal and standard medicines is their reaction to side effects and combos. While all medical treatments can have side effects, herbal medicine often touts a lower rate of bad reactions due to the natural interaction of plant-based chemicals with the body's biology. However, herbal medicines are not without risk; mixtures with standard drugs and the potential for harm with certain herbs are problems that require careful management. While highly successful, standard drugs can sometimes lead to significant side effects or issues, needing additional treatments to reduce these effects. Patient input and the treatment relationship also change significantly between these two ways. Plant medicine often involves a more involved role for the patient, who may be pushed to join directly in their mending process through lifestyle changes, food, and plant treatments. This choice of the patient is a core idea of holistic medicine.

In comparison, traditional medicine can sometimes be more strict, focusing on following the treatment plan explained by the healthcare provider. The choice between natural and standard medicine does not have to be mutually exclusive. Integrative medicine is a growing area that mixes the best of both worlds, giving a more thorough approach to health and healing. This method sees the worth of standard medical treatments for certain illnesses while adding organic practices, including plant medicine, to support general well-being. In conclusion, the comparison between drugs and traditional medicine shows a complicated world of healing practices, each with its strengths and limits. Understanding these differences is essential for people looking to make intelligent decisions about their health care, whether they are drawn to the overall approach of plant medicine, the focused methods of traditional medicine, or a mix of both. As the conversation between these two ways grows, it offers more specialized, effective, and complete patient care worldwide.

Harvesting and saving herbs are critical skills for anyone looking to utilize the natural healing properties of plants. The strength of a herb is highly dependent on how it is picked and kept, making these processes as important as the application of the herbs themselves. Proper packing ensures that the plant's vital energies and chemical elements are at their peak, while effective storing ways keep these qualities until the herb is ready to be used. When picking flowers, time is everything. The best time of day is in the morning after the dew has cleared but before the sun becomes too hot. This time ensures that the plants are not weakened from the heat and that their essential oils, responsible for their healing qualities, are at their highest concentration. The plant's growth phase also plays a vital part in choosing the best time for picking. Leaves should be taken before the plant blooms when the plant's energy is focused on leaf growth. Flowers are best taken just as they open, roots in the autumn when the plant's energy has returned to the root, and seeds when fully grown, but before they are spread—the way of picking changes with the part of the plant being taken. Leaves and flowers can often be gently plucked by hand or with scissors, roots may require digging, and seeds may need to be shaken or tapped from the plant. Regardless of the way, it is important to gather with care, taking only what is needed and leaving enough for the plant to continue to grow. This natural method ensures that the plants will be available for future gatherings and keeps the balance of the environment. Once gathered, herbs must be kept to keep their healing powers. Drying is the most common way of preservation and can be done using several steps. Air drying is the easiest and includes hanging bunches of herbs in a warm, dry, well-ventilated room away from direct sunlight. This method is suitable for most green veggies and flowers. For roots, seeds, or thicker parts of plants, oven drying or dehydration may be necessary to ensure complete drying without mould growth. The key to successful drying is removing wetness as quickly as possible without burning the herbs, which can lead to losing powerful oils and strength. After drying, herbs should be kept in covered cases away from light, heat, and moisture. Glass jars with tight-fitting lids are best, but paper bags or cloth sacks can also be used for short-term keeping. Labelling each jar with the herb's name and the date of picking or drying is crucial for tracking the strength and ensuring that the herbs are used within their ideal period. In addition to drying, other storing ways include freezing, making herbal oils, medicines, or spoonfuls of vinegar, and containing powdered herbs. Each method has its perks and is suited to different herbs and uses. Freezing, for example, is excellent for saving the taste and colour of edible flowers. At the same time, drugs and oils remove and focus on the medicinal qualities of herbs, making them more powerful and longer-lasting. The art of gathering and saving herbs is a rewarding practice that ties us to the natural world and allows us to take control of our health and well-being. With a bit of knowledge and care, anyone can make and keep their plant drugs, ensuring that the old wisdom of herbalism continues to live in modern times.

ESSENTIAL PLANT HARVESTING TECHNIQUES

Harvesting herbs successfully requires knowing each plant's unique needs and traits to ensure the best strength and medical value. The process starts with recognizing the best time for picking, which changes based on the part of the plant being used—leaves, flowers, roots, or seeds. Each part has a peak time during which its medicine chemicals are most concentrated. For leaves, it's usually just before the plant flowers when the plant's energy is focused on its growth. Flowers should be picked when fully open but not wilted, usually in the morning after the dew has cleared. Roots are best gathered in the fall when the plant's energy returns to the roots after the growing cycle. Seeds require patience, as they should be collected when fully grown but before they are spread by wind or wildlife. The way of gathering is equally important.

Leaves and flowers can often be picked by hand, gently pulling to avoid hurting the plant. Scissors or shears may be used for more rigid stems. Using clean, sharp tools to make clean cuts that the plant can heal from more easily lowers the disease risk. When gathering roots, a digging fork is often the best tool, allowing you to loosen the dirt around the roots without cutting them unnecessarily. Once lifted from the earth, roots should be shaken or brushed free of dirt and washed only if necessary, as water can remove some surface chemicals. The state of the plant at the time of picking is also essential. Only healthy plants should be gathered, as sick or pest-infested plants may have reduced healing properties.

Additionally, learning about the plant's presence and respecting its growth can help with healthy collecting methods. This means taking only what you need and ensuring that enough plant material is left to allow the plant to continue to grow and spread. After picking, the quick treatment of the plant material can significantly affect its quality. If not handled directly, herbs should be put in a box or laid out in a single layer on a clean surface, avoiding crowds to prevent heat and moisture build-up, which can lead to rot. Transporting the gathered material to reduce damage and breaking is essential to keep the purity of the delicate oils and chemicals within the plant. The time of gathering linked to weather factors is another problem. Picking should be done on a dry day, as wet plants are more prone to mould and mildew during drying. However, extra care should be taken during drying to ensure proper air movement and avoid any moisture-related problems if you must meet damp conditions.

In summary, suitable gathering methods combine time, method, and post-harvest treatment, each tuned to the unique needs of the plant being gathered. By adhering to these principles, one can improve the medical worth of the gathering material, ensuring that plant medicine's old knowledge and benefits are kept and passed on. This careful attention to detail in the gathering process shows a deep respect for the plants and the repair they offer, representing the spirit of sustainable and ethical herbalism.

HERB DRYING AND PRESERVATION METHODS

Drying and saving herbs is an essential skill for anyone looking to harness the benefits of plant medicine in their daily lives. This process extends the shelf life of these valuable plants and focuses on their healing qualities, making them more powerful and effective. The key to good preservation lies in knowing the various ways available and picking the right one based on the unique traits of each herb. Air drying is perhaps the most traditional way and is best suited for herbs with low moisture content in their leaves, such as rosemary, Thyme, and oregano. To air-dry herbs, gather them in small bunches and tie the roots together. Hang these bundles upside down in a warm, dry, well-ventilated place away from direct sunlight. This method allows herbs to dry slowly and naturally, saving their essential oils and taste. Oven drying is faster for herbs with higher moisture content, such as basil, Mint, and lemon balm.

Preheat your oven to the lowest possible temperature, spread the herbs on a baking sheet in a single layer, and place them in the oven with the door open to allow wetness to leave. Check the leaves frequently to avoid them from burning. This method can take several hours but is more controlled and quicker than air drying. Dehydrators offer the most consistent results and are great for drying large amounts of herbs. Set the dehydrator to the lowest setting, usually between 95°F to 115°F, and spread the herbs on the plates in a single layer. A dehydrator's steady airflow and temperature control ensure that herbs dry properly without losing their colour or vital oils. Freezing is another effective way to keep the freshness and taste of herbs. This method benefits herbs that do not dry well, such as cilantro, parsley, and dill. To freeze herbs, wash and pat them dry, chop them finely, and pack them into ice cube trays with water or olive oil. Once frozen, move the herb cubes to a freezer bag for long-term storage. Microwave drying is a quick and efficient way for small amounts of herbs. Place the herbs between two paper towels and microwave them on high for 1 to 2 minutes, checking every 30 seconds to avoid burning. This method works well for herbs with low to medium moisture content and successfully keeps their colour and strength. Regardless of the way chosen, it is essential to store dried herbs properly to maintain their quality. Use covered vessels made of glass, clay, or metal, and sign each container with the herb's name and the drying date. Store the packages in a cool, dark place to protect the herbs from light and moisture, which can lessen their usefulness over time. By learning these drying and preservation techniques, you can build a store of dried herbs ready for use in drinks, drugs, and other plant goods. This allows you to enjoy the health benefits of plants year-round and links you to the old practice of herbalism, enabling you to take control of your health and well-being with natural, time-tested options.

HERB PREPARATION TIPS

Preparing herbs for use is crucial in adequately harnessing their healing powers. This process ensures that the active components within the herbs are kept and made helpful for medical reasons. Whether you're making a simple drink or a complicated herbal mixture, the preparation of herbs is an art that requires understanding and care for the plant's purity and power. Firstly, finding and picking high-quality herbs is essential. Look for bright, organically grown flowers free from chemicals and pollution. The usefulness of a plant can be lessened by bad growth conditions, wrong care, or extended keeping, so getting from trusted providers is essential. Once you have your herbs, cleaning them gently without taking their essential oils is the next step. A light rinse under cool water will work for fresh herbs, then patting them dry with a clean cloth. For dried herbs, ensure they are free from dust or dirt by lightly brushing them or giving them a gentle shake. The way of cutting or grinding herbs is also essential. Larger pieces are usually picked for soups or decoctions to keep the vital oils. At the same time, finely ground herbs are ideal for medicines or liquids where a more extensive surface area helps remove the active chemicals. Use a sharp knife for fresh herbs to avoid damage and a mortar and pestle or a grinder for dried herbs to achieve the proper consistency. Different ways apply to different mixes when working the Herbst water can be poured over the herb for drinks or preparations and left to steep. The steeping time varies based on the herb; delicate leaves may require only a few minutes, while roots and barks may need to boil for an extended period to release their full benefits. For making drugs, the herbs are generally macerated in alcohol or vinegar, which acts as a liquid to remove the active substances.

The amount of plant to fluids and the length of processing can significantly affect the strength of the end medicine, so following specific recipes or guidelines is crucial. Decoctions involve heating the herbs in water for longer, which is especially useful for more complex plant materials like roots, leaves, and seeds. This method removes the soluble active chemicals and is often used for making powerful plant drugs. Drying plants for keeping includes ensuring they are entirely free of wetness to prevent mould growth. Herbs should be stored in closed boxes away from direct sunlight and heat to keep their healing benefits. Lastly, learning the unique traits of each herb is essential for achieving its medical potential. Some herbs are best used fresh, while others strengthen when dried. Familiarizing yourself with the herbs you plan to use and respecting their unique qualities will help you to prepare and use them successfully. Following these guidelines, you can prepare herbs to improve their healing attributes and ensure their benefits are readily available for improving health and well-being. This careful preparation is a practice of herbalism and a process that ties us to the old knowledge of plant medicine, allowing us to accept these natural medicines into our modern lives with respect and usefulness.

HERBAL PREPARATIONS

Herbal preparations are the cornerstone of utilizing medicine plants for health and wellness, changing raw herbs into manageable and effective forms for healing. The art and science of making these mixes have been improved over millennia, drawing from a rich past of herbalism. This chapter goes into the practical aspects of making infusions, decoctions, tinctures, ointments, creams, and essential oils, giving readers the information to make their plant medicines at home.

Infusions and Teas

The goal is to use hot water to remove the medical drugs from sensitive parts of the plant, such as the leaves and flowers.

Preparation:

- Boil water.
- Measure the proper amount of dried or fresh herbs.

Materials:

- Dried or fresh herbs
- Boiling water

Tools:

- Teapot or jar
- Strainer or tea ball

Safety measures: Ensure the water is not too hot to handle.

Step-by-step instructions:

1. Put the leaves in the jar or mug.
2. Add hot water to the leaves.
3. Depending on the herb, cover and let it sit for 5 to 15 minutes.
4. Strain and have fun.

Cost estimate: Low

Time estimate:15 to 20 minutes. Safety tip: Don't use hot water on easily damaged herbs if you don't want to lose their healing properties.

Maintenance: Clean tools after each use.

Difficulty rating:★☆☆☆☆

Variations: Can be sweetened with honey or mixed with other herbal teas for different effects.

Decoctions

Objective: To remove the active chemicals from more complex plant materials like roots, leaves, and seeds by boiling.

Preparation:

1. Measure the amount of herb and water needed.

Materials:

- Dried herbs (roots, bark, seeds)
- Water

Tools:

- Pot
- Strainer

Safety measures: Monitor the simmer to prevent burning.

Step-by-step instructions:

1. Place the leaves and water in the pot.
2. Bring to a boil, then reduce to a simmer.
3. Cover and cook for 20-45 minutes, based on the stiffness of the cloth.
4. Strain and serve.
5.

Cost estimate: Low

Time estimate:45-60 minutes. Safety tips: Keep a close eye on the pot to ensure it does not boil dry.

Maintenance: Clean pot and filter after use.

Difficulty rating:★★☆☆☆

Variations: Decoctions can be increased by boiling longer and kept for later use.

Tinctures

Objective: To extract medicinal compounds using alcohol or vinegar as a solvent.

Preparation:

1. Choose your plant and solvent.
2. Prepare your herbs by cutting or grinding.

Materials:

- Dried or fresh herbs
- High-proof alcohol or apple cider vinegar

Tools:

- Jar with a tight-fitting lid
- Strainer or cheesecloth

Safety measures: Use in a well-ventilated area when working with alcohol.

Step-by-step instructions:

1. Fill the jar ⅓ to ½ complete with herbs.
2. Pour solvent over the herbs until completely covered.
3. Seal the jar and mark it with the date and contents.
4. Store in a cool, dark place, shaking daily for 4-6 weeks.
5. Strain the juice and store it in clear dropper cups.

Cost estimate: Moderate, depending on the cost of alcohol or vinegar.

Time estimate:4-6 weeks. Safety tips: Label jars clearly to avoid confusion.

Maintenance: Keep tinctures in a cool, dark place.

Difficulty rating:★★☆☆☆

Variations: Glycerin can be used as a non-alcoholic fluid, especially for children's medicines. Ointments and Creams

Objective: To create a topical preparation using herbs for skin application.

Preparation:

1. Infuse leaves in oil.

2. Gather beeswax or good vegan options.

Materials:

- Herb-infused oil
- Beeswax or vegan wax
- Essential oils (optional)

Tools:

- Double boiler
- Jars or tins for storage

Safety measures: Be cautious of hot oils and waxes.

Step-by-step instructions:

1. Gently heat the herb-infused oil and beeswax in a double pot until melted.
2. Remove from heat and let cool slightly.
3. If using, add essential oils for taste or extra healing benefits.
4. Pour into containers and let set.

Cost estimate: Moderate

Time estimate:1-2 hours. Safety tips: Use caution when handling hot oil and wax.

Maintenance: Store in a cool, dry place.

Difficulty rating:★★★☆☆

Variations: Adjust the oil-to-wax ratio for a softer or harder consistency.

Essential Oils

Objective: To explain the process of getting essential oils, which is complicated and usually needs specialized tools.

Preparation:

Essential oil extraction is usually done through steam distillation, a way best suited for pros with the proper tools.

Materials:

- Plant material
- Water
- Distillation apparatus

Tools:

- Distiller

Safety measures: Handling a distiller requires knowledge of steam and heat.

Step-by-step instructions:

Due to the complexity and tools needed, specific distillation processes are beyond the scope of home preparation and are not included.

Cost estimate: High

Time estimate: Varies widely. Safety tips: Professional training is recommended before attempting steam distillation.

Maintenance: Regular cleaning and maintenance of the distillation apparatus are required.

Difficulty rating:★★★★★

Variations: Hydrodistillation and cold pressing are other ways of removing essential oils, each with benefits and problems.

By learning these herbal preparation methods, readers can tap the healing power of plants and make drugs that support health and well-being. Each technique offers a unique way to connect with the natural world, giving a direct link to the old art of herbalism. Whether making a quiet drink, a powerful potion, or a healing lotion, these preparations allow people to change their approach to health, using the old knowledge of herbs to address modern-day diseases.

MAKING INFUSIONS AND TEAS: TECHNIQUES AND TOOLS

Infusions and drinks, praised for their therapeutic benefits, are essential to herbal medicine, giving a gentle yet effective means to tap the healing power of plants. Making drinks and teas includes steeping the sensitive parts of the plant, such as leaves, flowers, or light stems, in hot water. This method allows the water to take the plant's liquid substances, including essential oils, flavonoids, and other vitamins, making them readily available for the body to receive and utilize. To start making mixes and teas, choose high-quality, organic herbs. The choice of fresh versus dried herbs varies depending on availability and personal taste. However, having had their water content removed, dried herbs can give a more concentrated flavour and better medical qualities.

Preparation for Infusions and Teas:

1. Boil filtered water. The temperature of the water is crucial; while hot water is usually advised, some delicate herbs may require slightly cooler water to keep their healing qualities.
2. Measure the herbs. A general rule is to use one teaspoon of dried or two teaspoons of fresh herbs for each cup of water. Adjustments may be made based on personal taste and the amount needed.
3. Place the herbs in a pot, infuser, or French press. These tools help the infusion process, allowing the herbs to interact easily with the water while making it easy to remove the plant material from the liquid after steeping.

Materials Needed:

- Dried or fresh herbs
- Purified water

Tools Required:

1. Teapot with infuser, French press, or a simple jar and sieve
2. Kettle or pot for boiling water
3. Measuring spoons
4. Timer

Safety measures:

- Ensure the water is at a suitable temperature to avoid burning delicate herbs.
- Use glass, pottery, or stainless steel tools to prevent chemical leaks from plastics.

Step-by-step instructions:

1. Boil the water using a pan or pot.
2. Measure the right amount of herbs and put them into the mug, infuser, or French press.
3. Pour the hot water over the herbs, ensuring they are fully covered.
4. Cover the teapot or press and steep for the suggested time. Steeping times vary, but they are usually 5-15 minutes for leaves and flowers, while more complex parts like roots and seeds may not be suitable for simple brews.
5. After steeping, strain the herbs from the liquid using a sieve if necessary.
6. The drink or tea is now ready to be sipped. Depending on personal taste, it can be eaten hot or left to cool and poured over ice.

Cost estimate: Low. The main costs are the herbs and speciality tools, such as a high-quality mug or French press, which are reuse purchases.

Time estimate: Preparation time is minimal, approximately 1-2 minutes for measuring and adding herbs to the vessel. Steeping time ranges from 5 to 15 minutes, depending on the herb. Safety Tips:

1. Always check the temperature fit for the herb being used.
2. Be careful when touching hot water to avoid burns.

Maintenance: After each use, fully clean the teapot, infuser, or French press with warm, soapy water to clear any leftover oils or plant matter. Dry completely before keeping to preventmould or mildew growth.

Difficulty rating:★☆☆☆☆. Making infusions and teas is accessible to beginners and does not require specialized skills.

Variations: By adding different herbs, infusions can be altered to suit individual health needs or taste preferences. For example, mixing chamomile and lavender makes a soothing blend ideal for resting before bedtime, while peppermint and Ginger can offer stomach support.

Through the simple yet essential act of making and drinking liquids, people can connect with the old practice of herbalism, bringing the natural world's healing gifts into daily life. This practice supports physical well-being and gives a moment of stop, meditation, and a link to the earth's abundant resources.

DECOCTIONS: TECHNIQUES AND TOOLS

Decoctions are a traditional way of taking medicine from the more challenging parts of plants, such as roots, leaves, seeds, and stems. This process includes cooking these plant materials over time, allowing the water to combine with the plant's active chemicals. Decoctions are particularly effective for pulling the deep, vital essences from plants that a brew or tea might not fully catch due to their complex, woody nature. The goal is to break down the plant material to release its medicinal qualities into the water, making it a powerful and healing drink.

Objective: To produce a concentrated liquid extract from the stricter parts of medicinal plants by simmering them in water.

Preparation:

Identify and gather the plant material you aim to decoct. Ensure it is clean and free from any toxins.

Measure the right amount of water. A general rule is to use about 1 pint (approximately 500 ml) of water for every ounce (about 28 grams) of dried plant material or two ounces (about 56 grams) of fresh plant material.

Materials:

- Dried or fresh herbs (roots, barks, seeds, stems)
- Water

Tools:

- A big pot or saucepan with a lid
- Measuring cups or scales
- Strainer or cheesecloth Storage jar or bottle for the finished stew

Safety measures:

- Ensure the pot or saucepan is of good quality and does not clash with the herbs.
- Monitor the soup process closely to prevent it from boiling dry.

Step-by-step instructions:

1. Place the plant stuff into the pot.
2. Add the measured water to the pot, ensuring the plant material is fully covered.
3. Cover the pot with a lid and bring the water to a boil.
4. Once boiling, reduce the heat to a simmer. Based on the material's stiffness, allow the mixture to cook slowly for 20 to 45 minutes. More challenging things like roots and leaves may require a longer cooking time.
5. Check the water level occasionally, adding more if it drops significantly due to evaporation.
6. After boiling, remove the pot from the heat and let it cool slightly.
7. Strain the liquid through a filter or cheesecloth into a storage container or bottle, pressing or squeezing the plant material to remove as much liquid as possible.
8. Discard the plant material and store the tea in a cool, dark place if not used immediately. Refrigeration is suggested for longer keeping.

Cost estimate: Low. The primary costs involve the plant materials and tools that still need to be available.

Time estimate: Approximately 1 hour, including preparation, simmering, and straining.

Safety tips:

- Always watch the cooking process to prevent the soup from boiling over or drying out.
- Handle hot drinks with care to avoid burns.

Maintenance: Clean all tools and containers used in the decoction process thoroughly after use to prevent contamination or residue build-up.

Difficulty rating:★★☆☆☆. While the process is straightforward, attention to detail and patience are required to ensure a potent decoction.

Variations: Decoctions can be created to address specific health problems by mixing different herbs known for their combined effects. For example, ginger root, turmeric, and black pepper tea can offer better anti-inflammatory benefits. Adjusting the cooking time and water amount can also give various levels and ratios decoctions, ideal for different uses and tastes.

By learning the cooking method, people can unlock the full healing potential of medicinal plants and more lasting parts, making powerful treatments that have been relied upon for ages in herbal medicine systems worldwide. This method offers a valuable way to utilize all parts of the plant and ties us to the old practice of herbalism, where the natural world is both a source of health and a path to better well-being.

MAKING MOTHER TINCTURES: TECHNIQUES AND TOOLS

Mother tinctures represent the essential extracts in herbal medicine, working as a powerful liquid form of a plant from which different dilutions and preparations can be made. These drinks catch the spirit and full range of active chemicals within a plant, offering a handy and effective means for giving herbal treatments. Making a mother extract includes macerating the fresh or dried plant material in a liquid, usually alcohol, to remove the healing qualities. This method ensures that the vital elements of the plant are preserved, resulting in a powerful and flexible medicine that can be used alone or as a base for further dilutions.

Objective: To create a concentrated extract of an herb that preserves its medicinal properties for therapeutic use.

Preparation:

1. Select high-quality, naturally grown herbs to ensure the safety and strength of the medicine.
2. Clean the plant material, removing any dirt or waste. If using fresh herbs, allow them to wilt slightly to reduce moisture content, which can weaken the liquor.

Materials:

- Fresh or dry herbs
- High-proof alcohol (at least 40% alcohol by volume, such as vodka or brandy)
- Distilled water (if needed to adjust alcohol content)

Tools:

- Glass jar with a tight-fitting lid
- Scale or measure cups for precise ingredient ratios
- Cheesecloth or fine mesh strainer
- Amber glass boxes for storage

Safety measures:

- Work in a well-ventilated place to avoid breathing booze fumes.
- Wear gloves when handling fresh herbs to prevent skin discomfort.

Step-by-step instructions:

1. Chop or grind the plant material to improve the surface area for extraction.
2. Weigh or measure the herb and put it in the glass jar.
3. Pour booze over the herbs, ensuring they are fully covered. The amount of herb to alcohol changes based on the plant's water content; a common starting point is 1 part herb to 2 parts alcohol by weight for dried herbs or 1 part herb to 3 parts alcohol by volume for fresh herbs.

4. Seal the jar tightly and mark it with the date and contents.
5. Store the jar in a cool, dark place, shaking it daily to help extraction.
6. After 4-6 weeks, strain the liquor through cheesecloth or a fine mesh strainer into another clean glass jar, squeezing or pressing the plant material to remove as much liquid as possible.
7. Transfer the squeezed liquid into amber glass bottles for keeping, marking each bottle with the herb name and date of finish.

Cost estimate: Moderate, primarily for high-proof alcohol and quality herbs.

Time estimate: 4-6 weeks for maceration, preparation, and bottling time. Safety tips:

- Ensure bottles are labeled clearly to avoid misunderstanding other medicines or home beverages.
- Store medicines out of reach of children and dogs.

Maintenance: Store mother medicines in a cool, dark place to protect their effectiveness. Properly kept, they can stay helpful for several years.

Difficulty rating: ★★☆☆☆. While the process is straightforward, attention to detail in measurements and patience during maceration are crucial for success.

Variations: Vinegar or glycerin can be used as solvents for those avoiding alcohol, though the extraction may not be as strong. Different herbs can be mixed in a single mixture for specific medical benefits, but understanding plant traits is encouraged to ensure stability and safety.

Mother medicines offer a creative and effective way to access plants' healing power, bridging the old practice of herbalism and modern-day herbal medicine. With careful preparation and keeping, these medicines can serve as a valuable component of a natural health program, carrying the spirit of the plant's medical qualities.

MAKING OINTMENTS AND CREAMS: TECHNIQUES AND TOOLS

Ointments and creams are semi-solid mixes used for external application to the skin, meant to deliver medicine herbs straight to particular body parts. These topical formulations mix the healing powers of herbs with a base that allows for easy application and absorption. The main difference between ointments and creams is in their makeup; ointments are oil-based and have more oil, making them greasier and more suitable for dry skin conditions. Creams are emulsions that contain a mix of oil and water, making them lighter and more easily absorbed by the skin. Making ointments and creams includes putting herbs into oil to remove their medical qualities, mixing this mixture with beeswax or a vegan wax to create a salve, or emulsifying the infused oil with water to make a cream.

Objective: To create herbal ointments and creams for topical application, harnessing the medicinal properties of specific herbs to address various skin conditions and support skin health.

Preparation:

1. Select and make the herbs based on the desired healing effect.
2. Infuse the leaves into a neutral oil.
3. Choose between making a balm or a cream based on the planned use and desired smoothness.

Materials:

- Dried or fresh herbs

- Carrier oil (e.g., olive oil, coconut oil, almond oil)
- Beeswax or veggie wax (for ointments)
- Distilled water or plant tea (for creams)
- Essential oils (recommended for extra medicinal effects and smell)
- Preservative (optional, for creams to increase shelf life)

Tools:

- Double boiler
- Strainer or cheesecloth
- Mixing bowl
- Electric mixer or blender (for creams)
- Spatula
- Jars or tins for storage

Safety measures:

- Ensure all tools and objects are thoroughly cleaned and sterilized to prevent contamination.
- Perform a skin test with the finished product to check for any allergic response before general use. Step-by-step instructions:

For Ointments:

1. Gently heat the herb-infused oil and beeswax in a double pot until the beeswax is fully melted.
2. Remove from heat and let cool slightly. If using, add essential oils at this step.
3. Stir thoroughly to ensure a uniform mix.
4. Pour the mixture into prepared jars or tins.
5. Allow to cool and harden before closing with lids.

For Creams:

1. Prepare the oil phase by slowly cooking the herb-infused oil and beeswax in a double pot until the beeswax melts.
2. Prepare the water step by heating pure or herbal tea in a different container.
3. Slowly pour the water phase into the oil phase while constantly mixing with an electric mixer or blender to make a mixture.
4. Continue to mix until the combination cools and thickens.
5. Add essential oils and thickener when the mixture is cool but still pourable.
6. Pour the cream into ready jars.
7. Allow to cool completely before closing with lids.

Cost estimate: Moderate, depending on the choice of herbs, carrier oils, and whether organic or high-quality materials are used.

Time estimate:1-2 hours, including preparation, cooking, and cooling times.

Safety tips:

- Be careful when handling hot oils and waxes to avoid burns.
- Label jars with the product name and date of production.

Maintenance: Store ointments and creams in a cool, dry place. Creams containing water should be used within a few weeks unless a preservative is added, in which case, follow the preservation rules for shelf life.

Difficulty rating:★★☆☆☆ for ointments; ★★★☆☆ for creams due to the additional steps required to create an emulsion.

Variations: Customize the plant mix based on specific skin needs, such as chamomile for resting, tea tree for its antibiotic qualities, or lavender for its calming effect.

Changing the amount of oil to water for creams can make lighter or thicker layers to suit different skin types.

MAKING ESSENTIAL OILS: BASICS, TECHNIQUES, AND TOOLS

Essential oils are pure plant goods that keep the natural smell and taste, or "essence," of their source. They are obtained through distillation (via steam and water) or mechanical, such as cold pressing. Once the scent chemicals have been removed, they are mixed with a carrier oil to make a product ready for use. The process of making essential oils is both an art and a science, needing accuracy and care to catch the powerful therapeutic qualities of plants.

Objective: To separate and concentrate the chemical molecules from plants, making essential oils that can be used for healing, medical reasons, or personal care items.

Preparation:

1. Select high-quality, healthy plant stuff. The choice of plant material will depend on the desired essential oil.
2. Clean the plant material to remove any dirt or trash.

Materials:

- Fresh or dried plant stuff (flowers, leaves, bark, or roots)
- Water (for steam distillation)
- Carrier oil (for cold pressing if making a ready-to-use product)

Tools:

- Distillation device (for steam distillation)
- Cold press machine (for cold pressing)
- Glass buckets for collecting and keeping the essential oil Labels for marking containers

Safety measures:

- Wear gloves and eye protection to handle plant stuff and tools.
- Ensure proper air in the area.

Step-by-step instructions:

For Steam Distillation:

1. Fill the brewing device with clean water and the plant material.
2. Heat the water to make steam. The steam will pass through the plant material, collecting the crucial oils.

3. The steam and essential oil fumes then pass through a cooling device to settle back into a liquid.
4. Collect the juice in a glass jar. The essential oil will separate from the water and be filtered or decanted.

For Cold Pressing:

1. Prepare the plant material by cutting or crushing it to show more surface area.
2. Place the prepared plant material in the cold press machine.
3. Apply pressure to remove the essential oil. Collect the oil in a glass jar.
4. If necessary, mix the extracted oil with a carrier oil to reduce.

Cost estimate: High. Distillation equipment and cold press machines represent significant initial expenses, and high-quality plant materials can be expensive.

Time estimate: The distillation process can take several hours, based on the amount of plant material and the unique extraction setting. Cold pressing is generally faster but needs preparation of the plant material.

Safety tips:

- Never leave the distillation equipment idle while in operation.
- Handle hot tools with care to avoid burns.
- Store essential oils in dark, cool places to protect their purity.

Maintenance: Regular cleaning and upkeep of the distillation equipment and cold press machine are essential to ensure they work correctly and safely. Follow the manufacturer's directions for cleaning and care.

Difficulty rating:★★★★☆. Making essential oils requires specialized equipment and knowledge of distillation or cold-pressing techniques.

Variations: Experiment with different plant materials to make unique mixes of essential oils. Each plant offers a distinctive scent, taste, and healing qualities, allowing for endless customization and exploration.

By learning the methods of steam distillation and cold pressing, people can make high-quality essential oils at home, getting into the ancient practice of removing plant essences. These essential oils can be used in various ways, from improving physical and mental well-being to giving green choices for personal care and home goods.

DOSAGE AND SAFETY

Determining the right amount of natural drugs is essential for their usefulness and safety. The strength of herbs can change significantly based on the species, where they were grown, and how they were picked and made. Unlike drugs with exact doses based on careful study, plant medicine amounts can be more complicated and customizable. It's essential to start with smaller amounts and gradually increase as needed and accepted, paying close attention to the body's effects. For most adults, beginning with the lowest recommended amount on product packages or from trusted sources and gradually changing is suggested. A popular drink starting point is one teaspoon of dried herb or one tablespoon of fresh herb per cup of water, boiled for 10 to 15 minutes. Tinctures usually begin with 1-2 millilitres, taken 2-3 times daily. However, these are general rules, and individual illnesses or plants may require changes.

Children, pregnant or nursing women, the old, and people with significant health issues should use herbs with care. For these groups, calling a healthcare provider or a trained healer before using plant medicines is highly recommended to avoid possible harmful effects or conflicts with drugs. Understanding the main concepts of herbs is critical to using them safely. Many herbs contain chemicals that can mix with drugs, change body processes, or cause reaction responses in susceptible people. For example, St. John's Wort can be combined with a wide range of drugs, including antidepressants and birth control pills, probably lowering their usefulness.

Similarly, plants like liquorice root can affect blood pressure and potassium levels, needing care for people with heart problems or those taking certain medicines. Awareness of possible drug-herb mixtures is essential, especially for prescription or over-the-counter drugs. Consulting with healthcare experts about all plant uses is crucial to avoid dangerous interactions.

Additionally, knowing and controlling side effects is an essential part of using plant drugs properly. While many herbs are well-tolerated by most people, unpleasant reactions can occur, including stomach upset, allergic reactions, or more severe effects based on the plant and individual sensitivity. In cases of bad reactions, stopping the natural medicine and getting medical help is essential. A detailed record of the herbs used, amounts, and side effects can help find the reason and avoid future problems. For those new to herbal medicine, starting with single-herb mixes can make it easier to watch the effects and spot any inadequate responses. Complex herbal recipes can be introduced once individual herbs are well-tolerated and their effects are known. Sustainable and responsible gathering of herbs is an environmental and social fear and a safety problem. Herbs growing in dirty places or taken from the wild without regard for sustainability can be infected with heavy metals, pesticides or weakened strength. Purchasing herbs from reputable sources that provide information on sourcing, gathering methods, and quality tests is essential for ensuring safety and efficiency. In conclusion, while herbal medicine offers a valuable addition to standard healthcare, respecting the strength and complexity of herbs is necessary for their safe and effective use. People can safely incorporate plant drugs into their health routine by starting with low amounts, calling healthcare providers, being aware of possible connections and side effects, and choosing quality sources.

HERBAL DOSAGE GUIDELINES

Navigating the world of plant amounts takes complicated knowledge that blends custom, science study, and individual health needs. The complexity of herbal medicine means that amounts can change significantly based on the herb, its use, and the person taking it. This guide offers a basic understanding of how to approach plant doses, ensuring safe and effective use. When considering the amount of any plant drug, the first step is to find the form of the herb. Herbs can be taken in various forms, including drinks, drugs, pills, powders, and oils, each needing different amount rules. For instance, drinks made from herbs are generally less concentrated than drugs or preparations, thus requiring a more significant amount to achieve medical effects. For herbal drinks, a standard amount might involve using one to two teaspoons of dried herb per cup of hot water, soaked for 10 to 15 minutes. This can be taken two to three times daily. However, more robust medicine teas might require more herbs or longer steeping times. Studying each plant individually is crucial, as some may require specific cooking methods to unlock their medical qualities or reduce possible side effects. Tinctures, alcohol or glycerin-based liquids of herbs generally come with a teaspoon for dose.

A standard starting amount is 1-2 millilitres (20-40 drops), taken two to three times daily. Again, the strength of medicines can vary widely, so it's essential to check the product package or a healthcare provider for help. Capsules and tablets offer a more handy type of plant diet but can vary significantly in strength. Starting with the lowest suggested amount on the product package is advised, and gradually raising it as needed based on your response. For many, this might mean starting with one pill or tablet, similar to 300-500 milligrams of the herb, taken with meals two to three times a day. When considering amounts, it's essential to consider individual factors such as age, weight, and health state. Children, pregnant or nursing women, the old, and those with ongoing health problems often require changed amounts and should visit a healthcare source before starting any plant habit. Interactions between plants and pharmaceutical drugs can also affect the right amount of a weed. Some herbs can raise or lessen the effects of drugs, needing changes to the plant or medication amounts. Consulting with a healthcare provider skilled in herbs and traditional medicine is crucial to handle these difficulties handlingsafely. Listening to your body is vital when playing with plant doses. Start with smaller doses and pay attention to how your body acts, changing as necessary. Some herbs may cause effects quickly, while others need to be taken regularly to notice the benefits. If dangerous effects emerge, dropping the amount or stopping the plant and getting professional help is essential. Remember, plant medicine aims to support the body's natural mending processes, not to overload it with significant amounts. By treating herbal amounts with care, respect, and a desire to learn, people can quickly adapt the healing power of plants to their health journey.

HERB-DRUG INTERACTION OVERVIEW

Understanding the links between plants and standard drugs is essential for anyone adding natural medicines into their health practice. Herbs, like pharmaceutical drugs, contain active chemicals that can affect the body in powerful ways. When mixed with regular medication, herbs can either boost or avoid the effects of those medicines, leading to greater efficacy, lessened effectiveness, or unpleasant reactions. This complexity shows the importance of treating plant nutrition with understanding and care. Many herbs mix with standard treatments by changing the body's uptake, handling, or removal of drugs. For example, St. John's Wort, widely used for its relaxing traits, can increase the processing of certain medicines, lowering their usefulness. This includes drugs such as warfarin, a blood thinner; birth control pills; and some HIV meds.

On the other hand, grapefruit juice, while not a weed, shows how natural substances can significantly affect medicine processing, leading to potentially dangerous amounts of the drug in the body. Cytochrome P450 enzymes in the liver, responsible for drug processing, are often the site of these interactions. Herbs such as Garlic, ginkgo, and Echinacea can trigger or stop these enzymes, changing the plasma amounts of drugs these routes process. This can require changes in drug amounts or, in some cases, avoiding certain plant products. Another area of worry is the risk of bleeding. Herbs like ginkgo, Garlic, and Ginger have antiplatelet traits, increasing the chance of bleeding with anticoagulant drugs such as warfarin or aspirin.

Similarly, plants that affect blood sugar levels, such as fenugreek, ginseng, and cinnamon, require careful tracking when used alongside diabetes drugs to avoid hypoglycemia. Blood pressure drugs can also be mixed with plants. For instance, liquorice can decrease the effectiveness of blood pressure drugs by increasing blood pressure, while hawthorn can improve the benefits of these drugs, possibly leading to hypotension. Given these challenges, people must talk to healthcare workers before mixing plant medicines with standard medications. This is especially important for those with ongoing health problems, pregnant or nursing women, and the old, who may be more open to harmful effects. When considering plant supplements, provide your healthcare provider with a complete list of all your drugs and vitamins. This includes over-the-counter drugs, vitamins, and plant things. Open talk ensures that healthcare workers can offer informed advice, helping to avoid possible responses and side effects. In conclusion, while plant medicines provide various health benefits, their combinations with standard drugs can pose difficulties. By learning these connections and speaking with healthcare professionals, individuals can easily add plant drugs to their health and exercise habits, enjoying the benefits of modern and traditional healthcare methods.

MANAGING SIDE EFFECTS

Recognizing and treating possible adverse reactions to plant medicines is crucial for ensuring safe and effective use. While herbs offer a variety of health benefits, like any healing activity, they can also cause side effects in some people. These reactions can range from mild to dangerous and may include signs such as stomach upset, allergic reactions, headaches, and dizziness. Understanding the possible side effects of plant medicine and how to handle them is essential for anyone using these natural treatments. The first step in reducing side effects is teaching oneself about herbs. Each plant has its own set of possible side effects and combos. For example, while Echinacea is widely used for defence support, it may cause allergy reactions in people sensitive to the Asteraceae/Compositae family.

Similarly, St. John's Wort, known for its calming qualities, can mix with a wide range of medicines and increase the chance of serotonin syndrome when paired with other serotonin-affecting drugs. It is also essential to start with low amounts of new plant medicine and raise to the suggested dosage. This method allows the body to adjust to the herb and can help lower the risk of harmful effects. Paying close attention to how the body responds to the herb is essential. If any toxic effects are noticed, dropping the amount or stopping the plant may be necessary. It's important to find high-quality things from trusted sellers when using plants. The quality of plant products can vary greatly, and contaminants or pollutants found in lower-quality goods may add to side effects. Choosing organically grown herbs and items that have been checked for quality can help reduce the risk of unpleasant effects. Stopping the plant and visiting a healthcare provider are advised if a negative response develops. For mild reactions, such as stomach upset, simple measures like drinking water, sitting, and consuming light foods can help ease symptoms. For allergic reactions, antihistamines may provide relief, but getting medical help is essential, especially if symptoms are severe. In cases where plants are used alongside regular drugs, being aware of possible interactions is necessary. Some herbs can increase or lessen the effects of medicines, leading to more fantastic side effects or reduced drug usefulness. Consulting with a healthcare source skilled in herbal and standard drugs can help handle these cases carefully. For people with ongoing health problems, pregnant or nursing women, and the old, extra care is suggested when using plant treatments. These groups may be more open to side effects and should always speak with a healthcare worker before starting any new plant treatment.

In summary, while plant drugs offer a natural approach to health and happiness, they are not without risks. By teaching oneself about the potential side effects of herbs, starting with low doses, picking high-quality products, and speaking with healthcare workers, people can safely incorporate herbal medicine into their health routine. Being careful in finding and treating possible bad reactions ensures that the benefits of plant drugs can be enjoyed without compromising safety.

HERBS FOR THE IMMUNE SYSTEM STRENGTHENING

Strengthening the immune system through medicine plants is a practice strongly rooted in the knowledge of old herbalism, showing a balanced approach to health and well-being that has been valued across countries and epochs. This method uses the power of plants to support the body's natural defences, giving a different way to current healthcare techniques. Echinacea, Astragalus, and Elderberry stand out for their usefulness and historical importance among the various herbs known for their immune-boosting features. Echinacea, a native North American plant, has a long history of use by old groups who noticed its value in treating different diseases. Its ability to boost the immune system has been the subject of numerous scientific studies, which show that Echinacea can reduce the length and severity of colds and other lung illnesses. This is credited to its complex mix of phytochemicals, which work synergistically to increase the activity of immune cells and inflammation responses that are vital in fighting illnesses. Astragalus, a Traditional Chinese Medicine (TCM) staple, is famous for its adaptogenic traits, helping the body fight stress and disease. It is thought to support the immune system by raising the production of white blood cells, which play a key role in protecting the body against viruses. Astragalus is often suggested for its ability to avoid upper lung diseases and to improve general energy, making it a key herb in the tools for immunity support. With its rich history of use in European folk medicine, Elderberry is praised for its strong antibiotic properties. The dark berries contain antioxidants and vitamins to help avoid colds and flu and lessen their length. Elderberry works by stopping the growth of viruses, thereby offering a natural means of defence against viral illnesses. Its broad success today, especially during cold and flu season, is a testament to its value and a long memory. Incorporating these plants into daily routines can be a simple yet strong way to improve immune function. Whether through drinks, drugs, or pills, the key is to pick high-quality, organically grown herbs to ensure the best benefit. It is also important to note that while these herbs can greatly strengthen the immune system, they are most successful as part of a general approach to health that includes a healthy diet, regular exercise, and proper sleep. Understanding each plant's unique traits and uses is crucial for improving its immune-boosting potential. For instance, Echinacea is most successful at the beginning of cold symptoms, while Astragalus is best used as a preventive measure during the change of seasons or in times of greater stress. On the other hand, Elderberry can be taken throughout the cold and flu season to provide ongoing protection against virus diseases. As we study the world of plant medicine, it becomes clear that the knowledge of old drugs gives useful insights into current health problems. Using plants for immune system boosting is a good example of how old practices can support modern medicine, giving natural, effective solutions for better health and well-being. Building based on immune support through herbalism, it's important to find additional herbs recognized for their health-promoting qualities. Garlic, Ginger, and Thyme, while widely found in restaurants worldwide, also play a key role in improving the immune system, each adding unique benefits to the table. Garlic, with its rich history in old countries, is a food staple and a powerful medicine plant. Its immune-boosting traits are largely linked to allicin, a substance released when Garlic is crushed or chopped. Allicin has been shown to display antibiotic and antiviral effects, making Garlic a strong friend against illnesses. Regular intake of Garlic can improve the efficiency of immune cells, helping to ward off colds and flu. Additionally, its defensive features help the general health and running of the defence system. Ginger, another veggie with a long history of use in different traditional medicine systems, including Ayurveda and Chinese medicine, offers major health support. Its main components, such as gingerol, have strong anti-inflammatory and antioxidative effects. These traits make Ginger an excellent treatment for reducing inflammation and improving immune response. Ginger helps ease signs of lung diseases, heal sore throats, and lower heat. Its warming nature also helps to boost circulation, further helping the body's ability to fight germs. Thyme is praised not only for its delicious traits but also for its role in immune system support. Thyme contains thymol, among other active chemicals, which have been found to hold antibiotic powers. This makes it highly useful in fighting lung illnesses, coughs, and asthma. Thyme's ability to boost immunity while easing signs of illnesses makes it a useful herb in avoiding and treating colds and flu. Incorporating these herbs into one's diet and health habits can be done in various ways, from adding fresh or dried herbs to meals to making herbal drinks and drugs. For instance, a simple tea made from Ginger and lemon can quickly ease cold symptoms. At the same time, garlic-infused honey can serve as a strong immunity booster when taken regularly. Thyme can be used to make a soothing tea or added to baths for a relaxing way to absorb its benefits through the skin. It's important to note that while these herbs offer significant benefits for immune support, they are most effective when mixed with a healthy lifestyle. Adequate sleep, a healthy diet rich in fruits and veggies, regular physical exercise, and stress control are all important components of a strong immune system. Furthermore, learning the right amounts and possible mixtures with other drugs is important for safe and effective use. Consulting with a healthcare worker skilled in plant medicine can provide specific information based on individual health needs and situations. The trip through herbalism shows a great trove of natural drugs that have stood the test of time. By accepting the power of plants like Garlic, Ginger, and Thyme, alongside Echinacea, Astragalus, and Elderberry, people can tap into old knowledge to strengthen and improve their immune systems. This full approach to health, which blends the best of traditional and modern methods, gives a road to better well-being and resilience against illness.

ECHINACEA: OVERVIEW AND BENEFITS

Echinacea, widely known as the purple coneflower, is a group of grass plants native to North America. This plant has been a staple in traditional Native American medicine for ages, known for its ability to treat different diseases. The use of Echinacea spread from native practices to become a cornerstone in plant care worldwide, primarily known for its immune-boosting qualities. The genus Echinacea comprises several species, but the most widely studied and used for medical reasons are Echinacea purpurea, Echinacea angustifolia, and Echinacea pallida. The plant is recognizable by its tall roots, which can grow up to four feet, and its unique purple flowers. The main components in Echinacea that add to its health benefits include phenols, alkamides, vitamins, and polysaccharides. These substances are believed to work together to improve the body's immune system, making Echinacea a popular treatment for avoiding and treating the common cold, flu, and other diseases.

Research into Echinacea's value has shown that it can lower the length and severity of cold symptoms at the beginning of sickness. This is credited to its ability to boost the immune system, raising the production and activity of white blood cells, which play a crucial role in fighting off illnesses. Additionally, Echinacea holds anti-inflammatory qualities, which can help ease pain and lower inflammation, further supporting the body's healing process. Beyond its immune-boosting benefits, Echinacea has been studied for its promise in wound healing due to its antibiotic properties. It can be applied directly to cuts and scrapes to avoid infection and promote faster mending.

Moreover, its anti-inflammatory effects make it helpful in reducing skin redness, making it a valuable component in treatments for conditions such as eczema and psoriasis. For those looking to add Echinacea into their health practice, it is available in various forms, including drinks, pills, medicines, and skin creams. While Echinacea is generally considered safe for short-term use, it is essential to speak with a healthcare worker before starting any new drug, especially for people with inflammatory diseases or those taking suppressing medicine, as Echinacea boosts the immune system. Incorporating Echinacea into a general approach to health, which includes a healthy diet, regular exercise, and proper rest, can provide an extra layer of support to the immune system. Its long history of use and the growing amount of study backing its benefits make Echinacea a useful flower in the goal of natural health and wellness.

EXPLORING ASTRAGALUS: USES & BENEFITS

Astragalus, known officially as Astragalus membranaceus, is an annual plant native to the northern and eastern parts of China, Mongolia, and Korea. This plant, deeply rooted in Traditional Chinese Medicine (TCM), has been utilized for ages to boost the immune system, protect the liver, and fight disease. Astragalus is marked by its long, thin roots, taken from four to five years old plants, reflecting the heart of the plant's therapeutic powers. The benefits of Astragalus are numerous, coming from its rich mix of saponins, vitamins, and carbs. These chemicals are credited with the herb's ability to boost the immune system, protecting against common lung diseases and colds. Astragalus achieves this by increasing the production of white blood cells, especially T-cells, which play a crucial part in the body's protection systems against germs.

Furthermore, its antiviral powers are highly helpful in avoiding and treating viral diseases, making it a staple in immune support practices. Beyond its immune-boosting benefits, Astragalus is respected for its adaptogenic qualities, helping the body fight stress and tiredness. This makes it a helpful partner in improving general health and energy levels, especially during greater physical or mental stress. The herb's ability to improve blood flow and its cardioprotective effects add to its status as a heart health boost. By helping in the control of blood pressure and giving antioxidant defense against oxidative stress, Astragalus benefits vascular health and avoids heart disease. Astragalus also plays a crucial role in liver defence, improving health and effectiveness. Its hepatoprotective traits benefit those exposed to outdoor toxins or those healing from liver damage.

Additionally, the herb's anti-inflammatory benefits make it an effective treatment for lowering inflammation throughout the body and easing gout and other inflammatory diseases. For those looking to add Astragalus into their health practice, it is available in various forms, including pills, drinks, and powders. It can be added to meals, made as tea, or taken as a supplement, giving a flexible and handy way to harness its health benefits. However, it is essential to speak with a healthcare worker before starting any new vitamin, especially for people with inflammatory diseases or those on immunosuppressive medicine, due to Astragalus's immune-stimulating effects.

In conclusion, Astragalus is a solid traditional and modern plant medicine shrub. Its wide-ranging benefits, from immune support and stress relief to circulation and liver health, make it a valuable addition to a balanced approach to health and fitness. By getting into the old knowledge of Traditional Chinese Medicine and bringing Astragalus into daily life, people can significantly improve their health and energy, representing the ideas of natural healing and preventive care.

ELDERBERRY BENEFITS AND INFECTION MANAGEMENT

Elderberry, officially known as Sambucus nigra, is a plant that has been respected throughout history for its healing powers. The elderberry bush's dark purple berries and flowers are rich in vitamins and antioxidants, such as vitamin C, flavonoids, and phenolic acids, which are known to boost the immune system and provide anti-inflammatory and antibacterial benefits. This makes Elderberry an effective natural treatment for reducing sicknesses, especially those affecting the respiratory system, like colds and the flu. The use of Elderberry in traditional medicine goes across countries, from Ancient Egypt, where it was used to improve skin and heal burns, to Europe, where it was considered a panacea for a wide range of diseases. Today, Elderberry is most widely taken in syrups, tablets, and pills, but it can also be found in teas and mixed into drinks. One of the critical benefits of Elderberry is its ability to shorten the time and lessen the severity of cold and flu symptoms. Studies have shown that blackberry chemicals can stop viruses' growth, keeping them from entering and attacking safe cells. This antiviral activity, mixed with the immune-boosting effects of its high antioxidant content, makes Elderberry a powerful tool in the fight against lung illnesses. Elderberry also boosts the production of cytokines, essential in the immune response, helping the body fight infections more effectively. Its anti-inflammatory features can help ease symptoms linked with colds and flu, such as fever, headaches, sore throat, tiredness, and muscle aches. For those looking to add Elderberry into their health practice for infection control, starting treatment at the first sign of illness is essential. Taking Elderberry within the first 48 hours of symptom development is most helpful in lowering the length of symptoms. While elderberry pills are widely available and generally considered safe for most people, it is crucial to stick to the suggested amounts and contact a healthcare provider before use, especially for pregnant or nursing women, young children, and individuals with inflammatory diseases. In addition to its antiviral and immune-boosting effects, Elderberry offers circulation benefits by helping to lower blood pressure and improve heart health due to its high antioxidant content. Its antioxidant features also make it helpful for skin health, protecting against UV damage and ageing. Despite its many benefits, it is essential to note that raw elderberries, as well as the leaves, stems, and seeds of the elderberry plant, contain cyanogenic glycosides, which can release cyanide, a deadly substance. Therefore, blackberry should always be eaten in its cooked form and never raw.

In summary, Elderberry stands out as a natural medicine with a long history of use in treating illnesses and boosting the immune system. Its antibacterial, anti-inflammatory, and antioxidant qualities make it a valuable addition to a balanced approach to health and exercise. It offers a natural way to support the body's barriers against common lung illnesses while offering more significant health benefits.

GARLIC: NAME, DESCRIPTION, AND BENEFITS OF GARLIC.

Garlic, adequately known as Allium sativum, is a species in the onion genus Allium. Its close cousins include the onion, shallot, leek, chive, and Chinese onion. This widely used medicine plant and food item has been a staple in human meals for thousands of years, with its roots going back to Central Asia and northeastern Iran. Garlic is famous for its unique taste and aroma, which can improve a wide variety of foods and its extensive range of health benefits. The bulb of the garlic plant is the most widely used part, split into numerous spongy parts called cloves. Garlic grows in many parts of the world and is a popular item in cooking due to its strong smell and delicious taste. However, beyond its food uses, Garlic has been known throughout history for its protection and healing properties.

Garlic's health benefits are numerous and have been backed by scientific studies. It is rich in vitamin C, B6, manganese, selenium, and other antioxidants, including allicin, the chemical responsible for its unique taste and many medical benefits. Allicin, made when garlic bits are crushed or chopped, has been found to have antibacterial, antiviral, and antifungal traits, making Garlic a natural way to boost the immune system. One of the most well-documented benefits of Garlic is its effect on heart health. Regularly eating Garlic has been shown to lower blood pressure in people with high blood pressure, reduce total and LDL cholesterol levels, and improve artery health. These benefits lead to a lessened chance of heart illnesses such as heart attacks and strokes.

Additionally, Garlic's anti-inflammatory traits help lower the chance of chronic diseases, including some cancers, by fighting oxidative stress and avoiding cell damage. Garlic also plays a part in cleaning by assisting the liver's function in removing toxins from the body. Its sulfur-containing chemicals trigger liver enzymes responsible for removing these substances.

Moreover, Garlic's ability to boost the immune system helps the body fight against colds, flu, and other illnesses more effectively. Studies have suggested that garlic supplementation can reduce the frequency of colds and speed mending time. For those looking to add Garlic to their health habits, it can be taken in various ways, from fresh pieces and pills to supplements like garlic extract and garlic oil. While fresh garlic pieces provide the best amounts of allicin, garlic pills are standardized to give a steady dose of this helpful ingredient without the garlic smell associated with its raw form. Despite its numerous health benefits, Garlic should be used with care by people taking blood-thinning drugs because it increases the risk of bleeding.

Additionally, some people may experience stomach pain or allergic reactions to Garlic. It is always suggested to speak with a healthcare worker before starting any new supplement habit, especially for those with present health problems or who are pregnant or nursing. Incorporating Garlic into the diet is easy and can significantly help general health and well-being. Whether used to improve the taste of foods or as a natural cure for different health problems, Garlic's flexibility and benefits make it a valuable addition to a healthy diet and an overall approach to health.

GINGER: NAME, DESCRIPTION, AND BENEFITS OF GINGER.

Ginger, officially known as Zingiber officinale, is a growing plant whose tuber, ginger root, has been widely used as a spice and traditional medicine. Originating from Southeast Asia, it has become a staple in many food styles worldwide, praised for its unique taste profile and its numerous health benefits. The root of the plant is where its strong properties lie, marked by its intense and spicy taste, which comes from its natural oils, the most important of which is gingerol. This chemical is responsible for much of Ginger's healing benefits. Ginger's health benefits are vast and varied, making it one of the world's most widely used food spices. Historically, it has been used to aid Digestion, reduce sickness, and help fight the flu and common cold. Its ability to ease nausea and vomiting has been particularly well-documented, including its success in treating morning sickness during pregnancy without the need for drugs.

Furthermore, Ginger has potent anti-inflammatory and antioxidant benefits, which can help lower oxidative stress due to having extra free radicals in the body. The anti-inflammatory benefits of Ginger can also lessen the pain linked with osteoarthritis. In some tests, those who took Ginger reported a significant drop in pain levels and disability. Additionally, Ginger has been shown to significantly lower blood sugars and improve heart disease risk factors in people with type 2 diabetes. This is especially important given the world's rise in diabetes rates and the look for food changes to support regular treatments. Ginger's effect stretches to its ability to help treat chronic indigestion, marked by repeated pain and discomfort in the upper part of the stomach. As it speeds up the emptying of the stomach, Ginger can be helpful for people having pain after eating.

Moreover, its warming qualities mean it can help boost metabolism and fat burning, a valuable tool for anyone looking to control their weight more effectively. For those dealing with monthly pain, Ginger is as effective as drugs like ibuprofen in lowering the level of soreness. Its painkiller and anti-inflammatory features make it a natural choice for women wanting relief from menstrual cramps. Incorporating Ginger into the diet is simple and customizable. It can be eaten fresh, dried, crushed, or as an oil or juice and is sometimes added to processed foods and goods. Ginger tea, made by steeping sliced or chopped fresh Ginger in hot water, is a popular and soothing way to enjoy its benefits, especially for gut health. Ginger can also be used in cooking, both in sweet and spicy recipes, giving a tasty and healthy kick to meals. Despite its numerous health benefits, Ginger should be used with care by individuals on blood thinners or those with gallstones, as it can mix with drugs and worsen certain conditions. As with any vitamin, it's suggested to speak with a healthcare worker before putting high amounts of Ginger into one's health program, especially for pregnant women or those with medical conditions. Ginger witnesses natural drugs' power, reflecting the goals of old knowledge and modern science. Its broad use across different countries and ages underscores its staying value as a powerful, natural means of improving health and well-being.

THYME: NAME, DESCRIPTION, AND BENEFITS OF THYME.

Thyme, known officially as Thymus vulgaris, is an annual crop from the mint family valued for its food, medicine, and beauty uses. This small, low-growing plant is marked by its woody stem, small, fragrant leaves, and groups of tiny, pale purple flowers. Native to the Mediterranean region, Thyme has a rich past that goes back to old societies where it was used for various purposes, including burying by the Egyptians and as a source of courage by the Greeks. Today, Thyme is praised worldwide for its unique food taste and health benefits. Thyme is rich in essential oils, the most important of which is thymol, which holds vigorous cleaning, antibacterial, and antifungal qualities. This makes Thyme an effective natural treatment for lung illnesses such as asthma, whooping cough, and sore throat. The plant works as an expectorant, helping to clear mucus from the lungs, and its antibiotic traits help fight the infection causing the illness. Thyme is also helpful for gut health; it can help ease gas and bloating, boost hunger, and promote efficient Digestion. Due to its high flavonoid content, Thyme's antioxidant traits protect the body against oxidative stress and inflammation. These vitamins can help avoid chronic illnesses such as heart disease and arthritis.

Furthermore, Thyme has been shown to positively affect blood pressure and cholesterol levels, improving cardiovascular health. For those looking to bring Thyme into their health routine, it can be used fresh or dried in cooking to add flavour to various recipes, including soups, stews, and marinades. Thyme tea, made by steeping fresh or dried thyme leaves in hot water, is a soothing treatment for coughs and sore throats. Thyme oil, taken from the leaves, can be mixed with a carrier oil and applied straight for its medical and anti-inflammatory effects, making it helpful in treating skin diseases and sicknesses. Despite its many benefits, using Thyme and thyme oil in balance is essential, as excessive usage can lead to damaging effects, especially in people with sensitive stomachs or allergies to plants in the mint family. Pregnant and nursing women should consult a healthcare worker before adding thyme pills to their diet. Incorporating Thyme into daily life offers an easy yet effective way to harness the herb's powerful healing qualities. Whether used in food goods, as a healing tea or applied directly in oil form, Thyme offers a natural, complete method to improving health and well-being. Its long-standing use in traditional medicine and ongoing acceptance in modern health practices underline Thyme's staying value as a flexible and helpful plant.

10 HERBAL IMMUNE BOOSTERS

Elderberry Syrup

Beneficial effects

Elderberry juice is famous for its immune-boosting traits. It is rich in antioxidants and vitamins that can help fight colds, flu, and inflammation. Elderberries have been shown to lower the strength and length of cold and flu symptoms, making this drink a go-to treatment during the cold season.

Portions

Makes approximately 16 ounces (about 475 millilitres) of syrup.

Preparation time

15 minutes Cooking time 45 minutes to 1 hour

Ingredients

- 3/4 cup dried elderberries (Sambucus nigra)
- 3 cups water
- One teaspoon dried ginger root or two teaspoons fresh ginger root, finely chopped
- One teaspoon cinnamon spice
- 1/2 teaspoon cloves or clove powder
- 1 cup raw honey (or to taste)

Instructions

1. Combine the dried elderberries, water, ginger root, cinnamon, and cloves in a medium pot.
2. Bring the mixture to a boil, then reduce the heat and simmer, covered, for about 45 minutes to 1 hour, or until the liquid has reduced by almost half.
3. Remove from heat and let cool until it is safe to handle.
4. Mash the berries carefully using a spoon or a potato masher.
5. Pour the mixture through a fine mesh strainer or cheesecloth into a big bowl. Press or squeeze the berries to remove as much liquid as possible.
6. Discard the elderberries and let the liquid cool to lukewarm.
7. Once the liquid is no longer hot, add the raw honey and stir until well mixed.
8. Pour the syrup into a clean glass bottle or jar.

Variations

- For a veggie version, replace honey with maple syrup or agave nectar.

- Add a tablespoon of fresh lemon juice for extra vitamin C and a tangy taste.
- Incorporate other immune-boosting plants, such as Echinacea or Astragalus, during the cooking process for extra benefits.

Storage Tips

Store the blackberry liquid in the refrigerator. It will keep for up to two months. For longer keeping, the syrup can be frozen in ice cube trays and then moved to a freezer bag for easy dosage.

Tips for allergens

You can remove or change them if you are allergic to any of them. For example, if you are allergic to honey, use the suggested vegan choices. Always ensure that the herbs and spices used are from sources that do not cross-contaminate with allergens.

Scientific references

- "Randomized study of the efficacy and safety of oral elderberry extract in the treatment of influenza A and B virus infections" by Zakay-Rones et al., Journal of International Medical Research, 2004.
- "Antioxidants from black elderberries inhibit the formation of inflammatory mediators in human monocytic cells" by Ho et al., Phytotherapy Research, 2017.

Echinacea Tincture

Beneficial effects

Echinacea powder is famous for its immune-boosting traits. It can help reduce the length and severity of colds and flu by boosting the body's defence responses. Echinacea is also known for its anti-inflammatory benefits, which help reduce symptoms linked to different inflammation illnesses.

Ingredients

- 1 part fresh Echinacea root, leaves, and flowers, finely chopped

- Five parts high-proof alcohol (such as vodka or brandy, at least 80 proof)

Instructions

1. Harvest Echinacea plant parts, ensuring they are clean and free from poisons or contaminants. If you need to grow your own, buy them from a trusted plant source.
2. Finely chop the Echinacea root, leaves, and flowers to improve the surface area for the extraction process.
3. In a clean jar, mix the chopped Echinacea with high-proof alcohol. The ratio should be 1 part Echinacea to 5 parts alcohol.
4. Seal the jar tightly and mark it with the date and contents.
5. Store the jar in a cool, dark place for 4 to 6 weeks. Shake the jar gently every few days to mix the liquids.
6. After sitting, strain the booze through a fine mesh strainer or cheesecloth into another clean jar or bottle. Press or squeeze the plant material to remove as much liquid as possible.
7. Label the end product with the date and ingredients. Store the liquid in a cool, dark place.

Variations

- For a non-alcoholic form, glycerin can be used as a replacement for alcohol, though the storage and extraction qualities may change.
- To improve the immune-boosting benefits, add other herbs, such as Ginger or Astragalus, to the liquor during the soaking process.

Storage Tips

Echinacea extract can last several years when appropriately kept in a cool, dark place. Ensure the bottle is tightly shut to prevent loss and breakdown of the active chemicals.

Tips for allergens

Individuals with allergies to plants in the daisy family should exercise caution when using Echinacea because of possible allergic reactions. Always start with a small amount to test for any bad reactions.

Astragalus Root Tea

Beneficial effects

Astragalus Root Tea is famous for its immune-boosting traits. It improves the body's response to diseases by activating and increasing the immune system. Astragalus is also known for its antioxidant benefits, which help protect cells from damage caused by free radicals. It has also been widely used to support heart health and improve general energy.

Ingredients

- One tablespoon of dried Astragalus root
- 4 cups water

Instructions

1. Bring the water to a boil in a medium-sized pot.
2. Add the dried Astragalus root to the hot water.
3. Reduce the heat and cook for about 30 minutes to allow the Astragalus root to absorb the water properly.
4. After 30 minutes, remove the pot from heat and strain the tea into a cup or mug, removing the Astragalus root.
5. Serve the tea warm. For extra taste, you can sweeten it with honey or add a bit of lemon.

Variations

- Mix Astragalus root with other immunity-supporting herbs such as Echinacea or Elderberry for a more significant health boost.
- To improve the taste, add Ginger or cinnamon during the cooking process.

Storage Tips

To maintain its usefulness, store any extra dried Astragalus root in a cool, dry place away from direct sunlight. Astragalus tea can be chilled for up to 2 days. Reheat gently before serving.

Tips for allergens

Individuals with allergies to plants in the Leguminosae family should speak with a healthcare source before drinking Astragalus root tea.

Garlic Honey

Beneficial effects

Garlic Honey mixes Garlic's antibiotic and immune-boosting benefits with honey's soothing and antibacterial effects. This treatment is helpful for colds, flu, and other lung illnesses. Garlic includes chemicals like allicin, which have been shown to improve the disease-fighting responses of some types of white blood cells in the body when they meet viruses, such as the viruses that cause the common cold or flu. Honey, on the other hand, works as a natural cough suppressant and can soothe sore throats, making this mix not only powerful for immune support but also for easing signs of sickness.

Ingredients

- 1 cup of raw, organic honey
- 10-12 cloves of fresh Garlic, peeled and finely minced or crushed

Instructions

1. Begin by picking a clean, dry jar with a tight-fitting lid.
2. Finely chop or crush the garlic pieces. This process creates allicin, Garlic's principal active ingredient.
3. Add the chopped or crushed Garlic to the jar.
4. Pour the raw, organic honey over the Garlic, ensuring the Garlic is fully covered to prevent spoiling.
5. Stir the mixture gently to ensure the Garlic is correctly spread throughout the honey.
6. Seal the jar tightly and store it in a cool, dark place for 3-5 days. This waiting time helps the garlic seep into the honey, boosting its healing effects.
7. After cooling, the Garlic Honey is ready to use. For health support, take 1-2 teaspoons of the mixture daily, especially during cold and flu season.

Storage Tips

Garlic Honey should be stored in a cool, dark place like a pantry or cupboard. Due to honey's natural defensive qualities, it can be kept for several months without freezing. However, ensure the lid is tightly shut to prevent moisture from entering, which could lead to fermentation or rotting.

Variations

For extra taste and health benefits, try adding other Ingredients to the Garlic Honey mix after the original 3-5 day soaking time. Ingredients like Ginger, lemon zest, or chilli pepper can improve the taste and provide extra immune-boosting effects. Add a bit of your chosen spice, stir well, and leave the mixture for another day before eating.

Tips for allergens

Individuals with allergies to Garlic or honey should avoid this treatment. For similar health benefits, try using a garlic tablet or manuka honey (for those not allergic to honey but wanting a different type). Always speak with a healthcare source before starting any new food product, especially if you have allergies or are taking other medicines.

Ginger-Lemon Immune Boosting Tea

Beneficial effects

Ginger-Lemon Immune Boosting Tea boosts the immune system by using the natural antiviral and antibiotic qualities of Ginger and lemon alongside the relaxing benefits of honey. Ginger contains gingerol, a bioactive substance with potent anti-inflammatory and antioxidant effects, while lemon is rich in vitamin C, known for its immune-boosting traits. Honey adds a soothing taste and extra medicinal benefits, making this tea an excellent treatment for colds, flu, and other immune-related issues.

Portions

Two servings

Preparation time

5 minutes Cooking time 10 minutes

Ingredients

- 1-inch fresh ginger root, thinly sliced
- One lemon, half juiced and half sliced
- 2 cups of water
- Two tablespoons of honey (or to taste)

Instructions

1. In a small pot, bring the water to a boil.
2. Add the sliced Ginger to the hot water. Reduce the heat and boil for 5 minutes to allow the Ginger to soak.
3. Add the lemon slices to the pot and continue to boil for 2-3 minutes.
4. Remove from heat and stir in the lemon juice.
5. Strain the tea into two cups, ensuring the ginger and lemon slices are removed.
6. Stir in honey to each cup while the tea is still warm, changing the amount to suit your taste.
7. Serve the tea warm for the best immune-boosting effects.

Variations

- Add a pinch of chilli pepper or turmeric to the tea for an extra health boost while it simmers.
- Replace honey with maple syrup for a veggie choice.
- Add a cinnamon stick during the cooking process for taste and health benefits.

Storage Tips

This tea is best served fresh but can be saved in the refrigerator for up to 24 hours. Reheat gently on the stove or enjoy cold for a refreshing immune-boosting drink.

Tips for allergens

Individuals with allergies to pollen may need to choose a different sugar than honey, such as agave syrup, to avoid possible allergic responses.

Scientific references

- "Antioxidative and Anti-Inflammatory Effects of Ginger in Health and Physical Activity: Review of Current Evidence"
- International Journal of Preventive Medicine, 2013.

- "Vitamin C and Immune Function"

Turmeric Golden Milk

Beneficial effects

Turmeric golden milk is a traditional Ayurvedic drink known for its anti-inflammatory, antioxidant, and immune-boosting benefits. This warm tea helps Digestion, improves sleep quality, and supports general well-being.

Portions

Serves 2

Preparation time

5 minutes Cooking time 10 minutes

Ingredients

- 2 cups of milk (dairy or plant-based)
- One tablespoon of turmeric powder
- 1/2 teaspoon cinnamon powder
- 1/4 teaspoon ginger powder
- A pinch of black pepper (to enhance absorption)
- One tablespoon of honey or maple syrup (adjust to taste)
- One teaspoon of coconut oil (for healthy fats and to aid absorption)

Instructions

1. Slowly heat the 2 cups of milk in a small pot on low to medium boil. Avoid boiling.
2. Add one tablespoon of turmeric powder to the milk as it heats.
3. Stir in 1/2 teaspoon of cinnamon powder and 1/4 teaspoon of ginger powder.
4. Add a pinch of black pepper. This is important as it includes piperine, which significantly raises the intake of curcumin, the main ingredient in turmeric.
5. Mix one tablespoon of honey or maple syrup to sweeten and one teaspoon of coconut oil.
6. Whisk the liquid slowly but thoroughly to ensure all ingredients are well mixed and the milk is smooth.
7. On low heat, continue to heat the mixture for about 10 minutes, ensuring it does not come to a boil but is warm enough for the taste to meld.
8. Once cooked through and thoroughly mixed, remove from the heat.
9. Strain the mixture using a fine mesh screen to remove big pieces and ensure a smooth look.
10. Serve warm in mugs.

Variations

- Vegan Version: Use almond, coconut, or oat milk instead of cow milk.
- Sweetener Variations: Adjust the amount of honey or maple syrup based on personal taste, or replace it with stevia for a lower-calorie option.
- Spice Adjustments: For a more decisive kick, raise the amount of Ginger or add a pinch of cayenne pepper.

Storage Tips

Turmeric golden milk is best enjoyed fresh, but if needed, it can be saved in the refrigerator for up to two days. Reheat slowly on the stove or in a microwave before serving.

Tips for allergens

Plant-based almond, coconut, or oat milk is great for lactose intolerance or dairy problems. Choose plain or unflavored types to maintain the original taste of the recipe.

Scientific references

- Hewlings, S.J., & Kalman, D.S. (2017). Curcumin: A Review of Its Effects on Human Health. Foods, 6(10), 92. This study explains curcumin's wide-ranging anti-inflammatory and antioxidant effects, backing its use in recipes like Turmeric Golden Milk for health benefits.
- Aggarwal, B.B., & Harikumar, K.B. (2009). Potential Therapeutic Effects of Curcumin, the Anti-inflammatory Agent, Against Neurodegenerative, Cardiovascular, Pulmonary, Metabolic, Autoimmune and Neoplastic Diseases. The International Journal of Biochemistry & Cell Biology, 41(1), 40-59. This thorough study shows the various healing potential of curcumin, including immune support, highlighted in the traditional use of Turmeric Golden Milk.

Reishi Mushroom Elixir

Beneficial effects

Reishi Mushroom Elixir is famous for its immune-boosting qualities, improving the body's resistance to infections and diseases. It also supports stress release, improves sleep quality, and promotes general well-being by managing the body's energy.

Portions

Makes approximately 2 cups

Preparation time

10 minutes Cooking time 1 hour

Ingredients

- 4 cups of water
- 1 ounce dried Reishi mushrooms
- One tablespoon honey (optional, for taste)
- One slice of Ginger (optional, for additional benefits)

Instructions

1. Combine the water and dried Reishi mushrooms in a medium-sized pot.
2. Bring the mixture to a boil over high heat, then lower the heat to low.
3. Allow the mixture to boil slowly for about 1 hour. Add Ginger to the pot at this stage if you're using Ginger.
4. After cooking, drain the juice to remove the mushroom pieces (and ginger slice if used). The liquid now is your Reishi Mushroom Elixir.
5. Stir in the honey to sweeten, if desired.
6. Serve the drink warm, leave it to cool and then freeze for cold intake.

Variations

- Add a cinnamon stick during the simmering process for a warming, spicy flavour.
- Include a bag of green tea for added antioxidants in the last 5 minutes of simmering.

Storage Tips

Store the Reishi Mushroom Elixir in a sealed jar in the refrigerator for up to 5 days. If you prefer it warm, gently reheat before serving.

Tips for allergens

For those with mushroom allergens, it's best to speak with a healthcare source before taking Reishi Mushroom Elixir. Honey can be removed or changed with maple syrup for a veggie choice.

Scientific links Studies have shown that Reishi mushrooms can control the immune system and have defensive properties. For instance, a report released in the Journal of Ethnopharmacology shows Reishi's ability to boost immune reaction. In comparison, another study in the International Journal of Medicinal Mushrooms describes its adaptogenic effects, helping ease stress and improve sleep.

Licorice Root Decoction

Beneficial effects:

Licorice root tea is famous for soothing gastrointestinal problems, including stomach sores, heartburn, and bloating. It also features anti-inflammatory and immune-boosting qualities, making it helpful for lung illnesses and sore lips. Additionally, liquorice root can support adrenal function, helping the body cope with stress.

Ingredients:

- One tablespoon of dried licorice root
- 8 ounces of water

Instructions:

1. Combine one tablespoon of dried liquorice root with 8 ounces of water in a small pot.
2. Bring the mixture to a boil, then drop the heat and cook for 10 to 15 minutes. The water should turn dark yellow or light brown, showing that the active chemicals have been cleared.
3. Remove from heat and strain the liquid into a cup, removing the liquorice root pieces.
4. Allow the juice to cool slightly before drinking.

Variations:

- Add a small amount of honey or a cinnamon stick during the boiling process for a sweeter taste.
- Mix liquorice root with ginger or mint leaves to increase its lung benefits.

Storage Tips

- The liquorice root tea can be saved in the refrigerator for up to 2 days. Reheat gently before eating.

Tips for allergens

Individuals with hypertension should use liquorice root carefully, as it can affect blood pressure levels. Opt for DGL (deglycyrrhizinated licorice) if afraid about these effects.

Scientific references:

- "The anti-inflammatory and immune-boosting properties of licorice root" Journal of Medicinal Plant Research.
- "Effects of licorice on relief and recurrence of peptic ulcer disease" World Journal of Gastroenterology.

Thyme Infusion

Beneficial effects

Thyme tea is famous for its strong antibiotic, antiviral, and antifungal qualities, making it an excellent treatment for improving the immune system. It can help ease signs of lung diseases, soothe sore throats, and promote general respiratory health. Additionally, Thyme is packed with vitamins, adding to its immune-boosting powers.

Ingredients

- One tablespoon of dried Thyme
- 1 cup of boiling water
- Honey (optional, to taste)
- Lemon slice (optional, for flavour)

Instructions

1. Place the dried Thyme in a tea bag or right into a cup.
2. Pour hot water over the Thyme, ensuring it's fully covered.
3. Cover the cup and leave the Thyme for 10-15 minutes. This helps the healing powers to be fully released.
4. Remove the tea bag or strain the mixture to remove the thyme leaves.
5. Add honey and a slice of lemon to taste, if wanted.
6. Drink the blend while it's still warm to improve its healing benefits.

Variations

- Add a slice of fresh Ginger or a pinch of cayenne pepper to the tea for an extra health boost during the steeping process.
- Combine Thyme with other immune-supporting herbs like Echinacea or blackberry for a more robust fix.

Storage Tips

The thyme blend is best served fresh but can be kept in the refrigerator for up to 24 hours. Reheat slowly without cooking to keep the healing benefits.

Tips for allergens

Individuals with allergies to plants in the Lamiaceae family (such as oregano, lavender, and mint) should continue with care when trying Thyme for the first time. Always start with a small amount to test for any poor reactions.

Oregano Oil Capsules

Beneficial effects

Oregano oil pills are a powerful plant treatment for improving the immune system. Known for their antibacterial, antiviral, and antifungal benefits, these pills can help ward off diseases and boost overall health. Oregano oil is also known for its antioxidant content, which can help remove free radicals and support the body's protection systems.

Ingredients

- High-quality oregano essential oil
- Cold-pressed olive oil or coconut oil (as a carrier oil)
- Vegetarian or gelatin capsule shells

Instructions

1. Begin by mixing the oregano essential oil with a neutral oil. A suggested amount is 1 part oregano oil to 3 parts carrier oil to ensure safety and lessen pain.
2. Once the oils are mixed thoroughly, carefully fill each pill shell with the oil mixture using a pipette or dropper. Avoid overfilling to avoid leaks.
3. Secure the top of the capsule shell to seal the oil mixture inside.
4. Store the whole pills in a cool, dark place to maintain their usefulness.

Portions

This preparation will yield approximately 30 capsules, depending on the size of the capsule shells used.

Preparation time

The total

Preparation time

is around 30 minutes, including the time needed to mix the oils and fill the capsules.

Storage Tips

Keep the oregano oil pills in a dark, covered container to protect them from light and air contact. Storing them in the refrigerator can extend their shelf life.

Tips for allergens

For those with reactions to coconut or olive oil, try using another safe carrier oil that fits your needs. Always perform a spot test when trying a new carrier oil to ensure no allergy reaction.

Variations

To cater to different health needs, you can mix oregano oil with other essential oils known for their immune-boosting qualities, such as lemon, eucalyptus, or frankincense oil. Adjust the ratio of oregano oil to neutral oil as needed to handle the addition of other essential oils.

HERBS FOR IMPROVING DIGESTION

Digestive health is a cornerstone of general well-being, deeply rooted in the old knowledge of plant medicine. Across countries and ages, different herbs have been respected for their taste, cooking contributions, and powerful stomach benefits. These natural methods offer gentle yet effective ways to improve gut function, ease pain, and promote the body's internal healing ability. Peppermint, known as Mentha piperita, stands out for its healing effects on the stomach system. Its main ingredient, menthol, calms the digestive system's muscles, lowering cramps and pain connected with indigestion and gas. Peppermint tea is a simple and lovely way to bring this plant into your routine, giving relief from bloating and an upset stomach. Ginger, or Zingiber officinale, is another powerhouse of gut health, praised for its anti-inflammatory and antioxidative traits. It boosts Digestion, increases saliva flow, and helps move food through the stomach system more effectively.

Ginger can be eaten fresh, dried, or as a tea, making it a flexible addition to your food and health tools. With its unique liquorice-like taste, Fennel has been used to treat different stomach issues since ancient times. Fennel seeds contain anethole, a chemical that can help relax the stomach and gut, lowering gas, bloating, and stomach cramps. A simple fennel tea or chewing on fennel seeds after a meal can be highly effective for stomach relief. Chamomile, known officially as Matricaria chamomilla, is not just for ease and sleep. Its antispasmodic and anti-inflammatory features make it a gentle treatment for soothing an upset stomach, lowering sickness, and easing gastric disorders. A lovely chamomile tea can support gut health while calming the mind. Aloe Vera, a fleshy plant, gives more than just direct benefits to the skin. When taken as a drink, it can help soothe the walls of the stomach and intestines, boosting the healing of sores and lowering inflammation in the gut system. Its natural cleaning features also make it helpful in easing constipation. Activated Charcoal, made from coconut shells or other natural sources, has a unique ability to bind toxins and gases in the gut, helping to ease bloating and gas. While not a plant, this natural medicine is included for its helping role in a balanced approach to gut health. It should be used carefully, as it can bind to nutrients and drugs, lowering their usefulness. Incorporating these plants into your daily practice can significantly improve gut health, but it's important to remember that balance is critical. Each individual's body acts differently, and what works for one person may not work for another. Listening to your body and speaking with a healthcare worker, especially when mixing herbs with standard drugs, offers a safe and unique way to better Digestion. Herbal medicines bridge the old world, teaching us the ongoing power of nature's pharmacy. By following these time-tested ways, we can easily support our gut health, tapping into our ancestors' knowledge to feed our modern lives.

PEPPERMINT ESSENTIALS

Peppermint, known officially as Mentha piperita, is a hybrid mint, a cross between watermint and spearmint, indigenous to Europe and the Middle East. Now widely spread and grown in many areas of the world, peppermint has a high menthol content, which gives a cooling feeling, a trait that separates it from other mint species. This annual herb grows in moist, shady places and can grow to about 30 to 90 cm tall. Its smooth stems, flexible roots, and dark green leaves with jagged ends describe peppermint and purplish, lance-shaped flowers. The plant's admirable traits are due to its essential oil, taken from the leaves and flowering tops. Peppermint's benefits are vast and varied, making it a staple in traditional and modern plant treatment. Its most notable feature is the ability to soothe the digestive system, making it an effective treatment for fatigue, heartburn, and irritable bowel syndrome (IBS).

The menthol in peppermint calms the muscles of the stomach system, easing cramps and pain.

Additionally, peppermint oil pills have been shown in clinical tests to ease greatly IBS symptoms, giving a natural and cheap treatment choice. Beyond its gut health benefits, peppermint includes antibiotic, antifungal, antibacterial, and anti-inflammatory traits. It can ease headaches and migraines as an essential oil mix on the temples and neck when applied directly. The cooling effect of menthol and its ability to improve blood flow to the area adds to its usefulness in pain relief. Furthermore, breathing peppermint essential oil can ease signs of phlegm and lung illnesses due to its expectorant qualities, making it a common ingredient in natural chest rubs and inhalants. Peppermint tea, made from the plant's dried leaves, is a popular herbal drink that offers the stomach benefits listed and serves as a cool, caffeine-free beverage that can soothe stress and improve mental clarity and energy levels. The smell of peppermint has been found to improve memory and increase attention, making it a helpful aid in study and job settings. Incorporating peppermint into one's daily routine can be done in various ways, from eating it as a tea or pill to using the essential oil for direct application or breathing. However, it's important to note that while peppermint offers numerous health benefits, it should be used with care. Peppermint oil is highly concentrated and should be softened before direct use to avoid skin pain.

Additionally, people with gastroesophageal reflux disease (GERD) or hiatal hernia may find that peppermint can worsen their symptoms due to its relaxed effect on the lower oesophagal membrane.

In summary, peppermint's flexibility and wide range of healing traits make it a helpful flower in natural medicine. Its ability to address various health issues, from stomach problems to pain relief and lung health, underscores the ongoing power of plant medicines in improving well-being. As with any plant treatment, speaking with a healthcare worker before adding peppermint to your health program is suggested, especially if you have current health problems or are taking medicine.

GINGER: NAME, DESCRIPTION, AND BENEFITS OF GINGER.

Ginger, officially known as Zingiber officinale, is a growing plant whose base, ginger root, has been widely used for its cooking and healing benefits. Originating from Southeast Asia, it has been a staple in traditional health systems such as Ayurveda and Chinese health for thousands of years. The root is marked by its robust and spicy taste and aroma, credited to its natural oils, the most important of which is gingerol. This ingredient is responsible for much of Ginger's healing qualities, including its anti-inflammatory and antioxidant benefits. The health benefits of Ginger are vast and backed by both past usage and present scientific studies. It is best known for its stomach benefits, especially ease of sickness and puking. This has made it a famous natural cure for morning sickness during pregnancy, as well as for nausea caused by chemotherapy or surgery. Ginger's speed in this area is so well-regarded that it has been the subject of numerous studies that have proven its benefits. Beyond its stomach support, Ginger has been shown to have a good effect on pain and inflammation. Its anti-inflammatory benefits make it a reasonable choice for reducing joint pain, menstrual pain, and exercise-induced muscle soreness. Some studies show that Ginger can be as effective as over-the-counter pain drugs for certain types of pain without the linked risks of side effects. Ginger also plays a role in blood health. Its components may help lower blood pressure, reduce cholesterol levels, and avoid blood clotting, lowering the risk of heart disease.

The antioxidant benefits of Ginger can further protect against different types of oxidative stress, adding to general heart health. It can be taken in various ways for those looking to add Ginger to their health habits. Fresh ginger root can be used in cooking or made into tea, while powdered Ginger is a handy choice for adding to soups, baked goods, and spice mixes. Ginger pills are offered for those needing a more potent dose. However, it's essential to speak with a healthcare provider before starting any new drug, especially for people on medicine or those with health problems. In addition to its internal uses, Ginger has benefits in beauty, thanks to its antioxidant and anti-inflammatory traits. It can help soothe pimples, promote a healthy look, and even add to skin repair. Despite its many benefits, Ginger should be used with consideration of individual tolerance levels and possible responses to drugs. While usually safe for most people, taking significant amounts can lead to stomach pain in some. As with any plant medicine, balance is essential, and Ginger should be part of a controlled approach to health and exercise. Ginger's continued success in cooking and medical situations is proof of its various benefits. Its ability to support gut health, ease pain, and contribute to cardiovascular and general wellness makes it a valuable addition to a natural health kit.

FENNEL: BENEFITS AND GI DISORDER REMEDIES

Fennel, officially known as Foeniculum vulgare, is a delicious food herb and medicine plant with a rich history from ancient times. Recognized by its tall, fluffy leaves and unique yellow flowers, Fennel is native to the Mediterranean region but has since been naturalized in many parts of the world. Its use covers different countries for cooking, medical, and holy reasons. The plant's bulb, stalks, and seeds are all edible, giving a sweet, anise-like taste that improves many recipes. The medical benefits of Fennel are mainly pulled from its seeds, which contain a potent mix of phytonutrients, including anethole, fenchone, and estragole. These chemicals are charged with Fennel's antispasmodic, anti-inflammatory, and antibiotic properties, making it a valuable treatment for different stomach problems. Fennel seeds are famous for easing stomach discomforts such as gas, bloating, and cramps. This is credited to their carminative effect, which aids in releasing gas from the stomach, reducing bloating and stopping the formation of additional gas.

Moreover, fennel seeds have been found to boost Digestion and improve gut enzyme activity, which can help improve general Digestion and food intake. Their antispasmodic benefits also ease the smooth muscles of the gut system, easing cramps and pain linked with conditions like irritable bowel syndrome (IBS).

Additionally, Fennel's mild, watery action can help cleanse the body and reduce water buildup, further supporting gut health. For people looking to add Fennel to their diet for stomach relief, a simple and effective way is to prepare fennel tea. This can be done by steeping crushed fennel seeds in hot water for 5 to 10 minutes, allowing the volatile oils and healing chemicals to seep into the water. Drinking fennel tea can quickly relieve gut pain and is gentle enough for frequent use. Another everyday use of fennel seeds is to chew them straight after eating. This practice not only freshens the breath but also stimulates the release of gut enzymes, promoting efficient Digestion and avoiding gas and bloating. For those who prefer a more helpful way, fennel pills are available in tablet or liquid form, giving a concentrated amount of the herb's helpful qualities. While Fennel is generally considered safe for most people, using it in balance is essential. Excessive drinking can lead to mild side effects, such as allergy reactions in sensitive people. Pregnant and nursing women should visit a healthcare worker before using Fennel as a fix due to its phytoestrogen content. Incorporating Fennel into the diet or as a plant treatment can significantly improve gut health, giving a natural and effective answer for reducing stomach problems. Its pleasant taste, freedom in preparation, and wide range of health benefits make Fennel a valuable addition to natural health tools, reflecting the principles of old plant knowledge applied in modern life.

CHAMOMILE ESSENTIALS

Chamomile, fully known as Matricaria chamomilla or Matricaria recutita, is a flowering plant belonging to the Asteraceae family, native to Europe and Western Asia. It has since spread to cold places around the world. Recognized by its daisy-like flowers with white petals ringing a yellow disc, chamomile has been a staple in traditional medicine for ages, valued for its healing qualities. The plant grows to a height of up to 30 cm and thrives in well-drained soil under full sun. Chamomile's success in herbalism is partly due to its variety and safety, making it great for a broad audience, including children and older people. The benefits of chamomile are numerous due to its rich mix of flavonoids, terpenoids, and other powerful phytochemicals. These chemicals add to chamomile's anti-inflammatory, antispasmodic, and cooling benefits.

One of the most well-known uses of chamomile is managing fear and anxiousness. Its mild calming action can help calm the nervous system, promoting resting and helping in better sleep. This makes chamomile tea a popular choice for those looking to relax at the end of the day or improve their sleep quality. Beyond its calm effects, chamomile is also praised for its stomach benefits. It can ease gut pain, reduce inflammation in the digestive system, and improve symptoms linked with conditions like irritable bowel syndrome (IBS), such as bloating and gas. The antispasmodic features of chamomile make it effective in easing muscle cramps and menstrual pain, providing natural relief without the need for drugs. Chamomile's anti-inflammatory and antibacterial qualities extend its use to skincare, which can help soothe sensitive skin, reduce redness, and promote healing. It is widely found in topical creams, ointments, and lotions for sensitive or problematic skin.

Additionally, chamomile's antioxidant content supports skin health by protecting against oxidative stress and lowering the signs of age. Preparing chamomile tea includes steeping dried chamomile leaves in hot water for about 5 to 10 minutes, which allows the healing chemicals to be released. Chamomile oil can be mixed with a carrier oil and applied to the skin, or chamomile extract can be added to baths for healing. While chamomile is usually safe for most people, it is essential to note that some individuals may experience allergic reactions, especially those sensitive to plants in the Asteraceae family, such as ragweed. Pregnant and nursing women should speak with a healthcare worker before adding chamomile into their routine due to limited studies on its benefits in these groups. Incorporating chamomile into one's exercise habit offers a natural, gentle way to support physical and mental health. Its long history of use in plant medicine and current research showing its health benefits underscores chamomile's staying value as a flexible and effective fix. Whether enjoyed as a relaxing drink, used in gut health products, or applied directly for skin care, chamomile shows the power of plant medicine to improve well-being and provide help for different conditions.

EXPLORING ALOE VERA: USES AND BENEFITS

Aloe Vera, known adequately as Aloe barbadensis miller, is a tropical plant species from the genus Aloe. Its leaves are thick and fleshy, green to grey-green, with some types having white flecks on their upper and lower stem surfaces. The tip of the leaf is sharp and has small white teeth. This plant has been used for ages for its health, beauty, mending, and skin care benefits. Aloe Vera grows mainly in the dry parts of Africa, Asia, Europe, and America. In addition to its broad use in the beauty, medical, and food businesses, Aloe Vera is also widely used in plant care. The benefits of Aloe Vera are numerous and various, making it a flexible plant for health and fitness. One of the most well-known qualities of Aloe Vera is its ability to ease and heal the face. This is due to the gel inside the leaves, which is rich in antioxidants, vitamins, and enzymes. It has anti-inflammatory and antibacterial traits, making it helpful in treating burns, pimples, and dry skin problems. Aloe Vera juice can also speed up skin cell reproduction as much as eight times, making it a powerful healing agent for sunburns and lowering the recovery period for skin injuries. Beyond skin care, Aloe Vera has been found to have several other health benefits. It includes chemicals known as anthraquinones, which are laxatives and can help treat constipation. The plant also has antiviral and antibacterial traits, which can help boost the immune system and fight off illnesses.

Aloe Vera juice is known for its healing features and can help fight hunger. Drinking Aloe Vera juice helps keep the body hydrated and offers a nutrient-rich source of vitamins and minerals, including vitamins B, C, E, and folic acid. Aloe Vera's effects spread to the gut system as well. The plant's relaxing features can help calm the stomach and intestines, promoting healthy Digestion. It is helpful for those with irritable bowel syndrome (IBS) and other inflammation diseases of the gut. Aloe Vera's prebiotic components can also help to promote the growth of good bacteria in the stomach, improving general gut health. For those interested in adding Aloe Vera into their health and exercise practice, it can be used in different ways. The gel can be applied straight to the face, or the juice can be eaten for its stomach and hydrating effects. However, knowing that Aloe Vera should be used with care is essential. When drinking Aloe Vera juice, it is crucial to ensure that the product is free from aloft, a substance found in the upper leaf that can cause harmful effects if taken in large amounts. Always speak with a healthcare worker before taking any new product, especially if you have current health problems or are pregnant.

In summary, aloe vera is a robust plant with a wide range of uses for health and exercise. It offers natural, practical answers for various health problems, from fixing sunburns and refreshing the skin to helping Digestion and boosting the immune system. Its long history of use in traditional medicine and growing amount of scientific study show its worth as a helpful addition to modern health practices.

ACTIVATED CHARCOAL: OVERVIEW & BENEFITS

Activated Charcoal, often taken from coconut shells, wood, or other natural sources, gets a unique process to improve its adsorptive power, making it highly useful for various medical and health-related uses. This type of Charcoal is handled at very high temps that change its internal structure, dropping the size of its holes and increasing its surface area. This results in a charcoal that is more porous than regular Charcoal, capable of adsorbing more toxins and chemicals. It's this unique feature that gives activated Charcoal its various health benefits, especially in the fields of cleaning and poisoning treatment. One of the primary uses of activated Charcoal is in the emergency treatment of certain kinds of poisons and drug abuse, where its ability to absorb chemicals can significantly reduce their uptake in the gut tract, thereby lowering their systemic effects. It's crucial, however, that it is given only under medical guidance in such scenarios, as its excessive use can interfere with getting helpful nutrients and medicines. Beyond its application in acute poisoning, activated Charcoal has found its way into general health practices. It lowers gut gas (flatulence), drops cholesterol levels, and even stops hangovers. However, the proof backing these uses varies, and while some people report benefits, scientific studies have only sometimes regularly backed these claims. Activated Charcoal is also popular in oral care, especially in natural toothpaste recipes, where it is charged with cleaning teeth by adsorbing germs and other chemicals that stain the teeth. Yet, users should continue with care, as its gritty nature can damage tooth enamel if used heavily. In makeup, activated Charcoal is added to masks and washes for its ability to draw out impurities from the skin. Its adsorptive properties are believed to help clear pores, remove extra oil, and ease acne signs, making it a preferred ingredient in natural beauty practices. Despite its various uses, the use of activated Charcoal comes with problems. It is not specific in what it adsorbs, meaning it can link to nutrients, medicinal drugs, and vitamins, possibly lowering their value. Therefore, it should be taken with a gap of at least two hours from meals or medicines to avoid unwanted conflicts.

Moreover, while activated Charcoal is usually considered safe for most people, it can cause side effects such as constipation or black stools. In rare cases, if eaten or taken wrong, it can lead to more significant problems, such as blockages in the stomach system. For those interested in finding the benefits of activated Charcoal, it's available in various forms, including pills, powders, and even as an ingredient in food items. However, it's essential to find things from trusted sellers to ensure quality and safety. Consulting with a healthcare source before adding activated Charcoal into any health program is recommended, especially for people with existing health problems or those taking prescription medicines, to handle its use carefully and efficiently. Incorporating activated Charcoal into one's exercise routine offers a natural choice for detoxing and cleaning, showing a more significant interest in tapping the power of natural substances for health and well-being. Its numerous uses, from emergency medicine to daily health and beauty habits, underscore the flexibility of this old cure, renewed in modern health practices.

TEN HERBAL REMEDIES FOR IMPROVING DIGESTION

Peppermint Tea

Beneficial effects

Peppermint Tea is praised for its relaxing effects on the digestive system, which reduces signs of heartburn, sickness, and irritable bowel syndrome (IBS). Its antispasmodic benefits help relax the digestive system's muscles, easing cramps and pain. Additionally, peppermint tea can relieve headaches and improve mental focus.

Ingredients

- One tablespoon of dried peppermint leaves or one peppermint tea bag
- 8 ounces of boiling water
- Honey or lemon (optional, for taste)

Instructions

1. Place the dried peppermint leaves or tea bag in a cup.
2. Pour the hot water over the peppermint and cover the cup to avoid the escape of burning oils.
3. Steep for 5-10 minutes, based on the needed strength.
4. Remove the peppermint leaves or tea bag from the cup.
5. If wanted, add honey or lemon to taste before drinking.

6. Enjoy the tea while it's warm to feel its full stomach and healing effects.

Variations

- For a cooling summer drink, leave the tea to cool and chill for 2-3 hours. Serve over ice.
- Combine peppermint with Ginger in your tea to improve its stomach benefits.
- Add a cinnamon stick while steeping for a warm, spicy taste.

Storage Tips

Dried peppermint leaves should be kept in a tight jar in a cool, dark place to keep their usefulness. Prepared peppermint tea can be kept in the refrigerator for up to 24 hours.

Tips for allergens

Individuals with allergies to menthol, a chemical found in peppermint, should continue with care. For those allergic to peppermint, try a softer plant tea, such as chamomile, for stomach relief.

Chamomile Infusion

Beneficial effects

Chamomile Infusion is praised for its calming and stomach benefits. It can soothe the stomach, ease indigestion, and reduce nervousness, promoting a sense of rest and well-being. Its anti-inflammatory features also make it helpful for lowering stomach pain.

Ingredients

- Two teaspoons of dried chamomile flowers
- 8 ounces of boiling water
- Honey or lemon (optional, for taste)

Instructions

1. Place the dried chamomile leaves in a tea bag or cup.
2. Pour the hot water over the chamomile flowers, ensuring they are fully covered.
3. Cover the cup and allow the chamomile to sit for 5-10 minutes. The longer it steeps, the stronger the mixture will be.
4. Remove the tea strainer or strain the chamomile leaves from the water.
5. Add honey or a bit of lemon to taste, if desired.
6. Enjoy the warm chamomile tea to feel its full stomach and calming benefits.

Variations

- Add a mint leaf or a slice of Ginger during the steeping process for a more complicated taste.
- Combine chamomile with lavender for an improved calming effect.

Storage Tips

Chamomile flowers should be stored in a cool, dark place in a sealed container to keep strength. The prepared chamomile tea is best enjoyed fresh but can be kept for up to 24 hours. Reheat gently without boiling to enjoy again.

Tips for allergens

Individuals with allergies to plants in the daisy family, such as ragweed, should exercise caution when trying chamomile for the first time. Start with a small amount to test for any bad reactions.

Fennel Seed Tea

Beneficial effects

Fennel Seed Tea is praised for its ability to soothe stomach discomforts such as bloating, gas, and cramps. Its antispasmodic features help relax the muscles in the digestive system, making it an excellent treatment for IBS symptoms. Additionally, fennel seeds contain anethole, which can lower inflammation and support healthy Digestion.

Ingredients

- 1-2 teaspoons of dried fennel seeds
- 1 cup of boiling water
- Honey or lemon (optional, for taste)

Instructions

1. Crush the fennel seeds softly with a mortar and pestle to release their oil and taste.
2. Place the crushed fennel seeds in a tea bag or cup.
3. Pour hot water over the fennel seeds and cover the cup with a lid or a small plate to trap the steam.
4. Allow the tea to steep for 5-10 minutes, based on how strong you prefer the taste.
5. Remove the tea sieve or strain the tea to remove the seeds.
6. Add honey or a bit of lemon to taste, if desired.
7. Enjoy the tea warm, best after meals for stomach benefits.

Variations

- Add a slice of fresh Ginger or a stick of cinnamon while steeping for a more complicated taste.
- Combine with chamomile or peppermint tea for extra digestive and relaxing effects.

Storage Tips

Store unused dried fennel seeds in an airtight container in a cool, dark place to maintain potency.

Tips for allergens

Individuals with allergies to carrots or celery, which are in the same family as Fennel, should exercise caution when trying fennel seed tea for the first time.

Dandelion Root Coffee

Beneficial effects

Dandelion Root Coffee is praised for cleaning, improving liver function, and helping Digestion. It works as a weak diuretic, improving kidney health and boosting bile flow, which helps break down fats. This green coffee alternative is rich in vitamins A, C, D, and B complex, minerals such as iron, potassium, and zinc, and antioxidants, making it a healthy way to start your day or enjoy a warm beverage without caffeine.

Ingredients

- Two tablespoons of roasted dandelion root
- 4 cups of water
- Optional: honey or maple syrup to sweeten
- Optional: milk or a milk alternative for creaminess

Instructions

1. Place the baked dandelion root in a pot and add 4 cups of water.
2. Bring the water to a boil, then drop the heat and simmer for about 10 minutes. The longer you boil, the stronger the "coffee" will be.
3. After boiling, drain the liquid to remove all the dandelion root pieces, putting the "coffee" into your cup or coffee pot.
4. If wanted, sweeten with honey or maple syrup and add milk or a milk alternative to taste.

Variations

- For a spicy twist, add a cinnamon stick or a few slices of fresh Ginger to the pot while boiling.
- Combine with chicory root for a richer, more coffee-like taste.
- Cool the dandelion root coffee for a cold version and serve over ice cubes.

Storage Tips

The dandelion root coffee can be saved in the refrigerator for up to 2 days. Reheat on the stove or enjoy cold. If you've made a significant amount, try freezing

Portions

for quick and easy preparation later.

Tips for allergens

For those with allergies or responses to dandelion, it's best to speak with a healthcare source before eating. However, as a naturally caffeine-free liquid, it's an excellent choice for lowering caffeine intake.

Lemon Balm Tincture

Beneficial effects

Lemon Balm Tincture is praised for its peaceful and healing qualities, making it an excellent cure for worry, stress, and sleepiness. It also aids in gut health, helping to ease signs of indigestion, bloating, and gas. Additionally, its antibiotic features make it helpful for healing cold spots and other virus sicknesses.

Ingredients

- 1 cup fresh lemon balm leaves, thoroughly washed and patted dry
- 2 cups high-proof alcohol (such as vodka or brandy, at least 80 proof)

Instructions

1. Finely chop or crush the lemon balm leaves to release their oils.
2. Place the chopped lemon balm in a clean, dry jar.
3. Pour the alcohol over the lemon balm, fully covering the leaves.
4. Seal the jar tightly and mark it with the date and contents.
5. Store the jar in a cool, dark place for 4 to 6 weeks, shaking it gently every few days.

6. After soaking, strain the liquor through a fine mesh strainer or cheesecloth into another clean jar or bottle, pressing the plant material to remove as much liquid as possible.
7. Label the end product with the date and ingredients. Store in a cool, dark place.

Variations

- For a non-alcoholic form, veggie glycerin can be used in place of alcohol, though the shelf life may be shorter.
- To improve the relaxing benefits, add other herbs, such as chamomile or lavender, to the tea during the soaking process.

Storage Tips

When stored properly in a cool, dark place, lemon balm liquid lasts several years. Ensure the bottle is tightly shut to avoid loss and breakdown of the active chemicals.

Tips for allergens

Individuals with allergies to plants in the mint family should take care when using lemon balm. Always start with a small amount to test for any inadequate responses.

Caraway Seed Infusion

Beneficial effects

Caraway Seed Infusion is known for its digestive aid qualities, which ease bloating, gas, and heartburn. It can also help boost hunger and ease the pain of heartburn. The carminative features of caraway seeds make this drink an excellent choice for improving digestion and avoiding gas formation in the gastric system.

Ingredients

- One teaspoon of caraway seeds
- 1 cup of boiling water

Instructions

1. Crush the caraway seeds softly with a spoon, mortar, and pestle to release their volatile oils.
2. Place the crushed seeds in a mug or a cup.
3. Pour the hot water over the seeds.
4. Cover and steep for 10-15 minutes.
5. Strain the juice into a cup to remove the seeds.
6. Drink the blend warm; it is best after meals to help digestion.

Variations

Add a teaspoon of honey or a slice of ginger while steeping for a sweeter taste.

Combine with peppermint leaves or fennel seeds to improve the gut effects and add a delicious taste.

Storage

Tips

Store extra caraway seeds in a covered jar in a cool, dry place to protect their usefulness. The Caraway Seed Infusion is best served fresh, but you can freeze the strained infusion for up to 2 days. Gently warm without cooking before drinking.

Tips for allergens

Individuals with a known allergy to caraway or other plants in the Apiaceae family should avoid this mixture. As always, if you're trying a new fix for the first time, start with a small amount to ensure you don't have an adverse reaction.

Marshmallow Root Tea

Beneficial effects

Marshmallow Root Tea is praised for its relaxing effects on the digestive system, especially in easing soreness and inflammation of the nasal membranes. It makes a covered layer on the digestive system's walls, helping to treat problems like gastritis, bloating, heartburn, and ulcers. Additionally, its expectorant features make it helpful for soothing sore throats and dry coughs.

Ingredients

- Two tablespoons of dried marshmallow root
- 16 ounces (about 2 cups) of boiling water

Instructions

1. Place the dried marshmallow root in a jar or mug.
2. Pour the hot water over the marshmallow root, ensuring it is completely covered.
3. Cover and steep for at least 4 hours or overnight for a higher dose. This long steeping time helps the mucilaginous properties of the root to be fully released.
4. Strain the tea to remove the marshmallow root.
5. If the tea has cooled too much, it can be warmed slightly before drinking. Consume 2-3 cups daily for stomach ease.

Variations

- Add a slice of ginger or a cinnamon stick for extra taste and stomach benefits during the steeping process.
- Honey or lemon can be added to taste, but remember that adding lemon may lessen the mucilaginous effect.

Storage Tips

Marshmallow Root Tea can be stored in the refrigerator for up to 3 days. Reheat gently on the stove or enjoy cold.

Tips for allergens

Marshmallow Root Tea is generally well-tolerated, but those allergic to plants in the Malvaceae family should approach it carefully. As always, speak with a healthcare provider before bringing any new plant medicine into your routine, especially if you are pregnant, nursing, or on medication.

Slippery Elm Bark Decoction
Beneficial effects

Slippery Elm Bark Decoction is famous for its relaxing effects on the digestive system, helping with conditions such as acid reflux, gastritis, and irritable bowel syndrome (IBS). Its mucilage content coats and protects the nasal membranes lining the digestive system, reducing swelling and pain. Additionally, it can aid in easing sore throats and coughs by giving a covered layer around the affected area.

Ingredients

- Two tablespoons of dried slippery elm bark powder
- 2 cups of water

Instructions

1. Add 2 cups of water to a small pot and boil.
2. Reduce the heat to low and gradually whisk in 2 tablespoons of dried slippery elm bark powder.
3. Simmer the mixture for about 10 to 15 minutes, stirring occasionally, until it thickens slightly.
4. Remove from heat and let it cool to an acceptable drinking temperature.
5. Strain the soup through a fine mesh sieve to remove any big pieces, if desired.
6. Consume the soup warm for the best benefits.

Variations

- For extra taste and stomach benefits, try adding a teaspoon of honey or a pinch of cinnamon to the drink after it has cooled slightly.
- Mix in a small amount of fresh lemon juice to improve its healing benefits on the throat.

Storage Tips

The Slippery Elm Bark Decoction can be saved in the refrigerator for up to 3 days. Reheat slowly on the stove or in a microwave before eating. Ensure it is stirred well before warming to spread any set pieces.

Tips for allergens

Slippery elm is usually well-tolerated, but people with a known sensitivity to elm pollen should continue with care. As always, speak with a healthcare source before adding any new plant medicine into your routine, especially if you are pregnant, nursing, or have existing health conditions.

Anise Seed Tea
Beneficial effects

Anise Seed Tea is praised for improving digestion, reducing bloating, and easing signs of indigestion and pain. Its natural antispasmodic benefits help relax the digestive system, making it an excellent cure for gas and bloating. Additionally, anise seed is known for its expectorant traits, helping to ease congestion in cases of colds and flu.

Ingredients

- One teaspoon of dried anise seeds
- 1 cup of boiling water
- Honey or lemon (optional, for taste)

Instructions

1. Place the dried anise seeds in a tea infuser or cup.
2. Pour hot water over the anise seeds, ensuring they are fully covered.
3. Cover the cup and leave the anise seeds for 5-10 minutes. The longer it steeps, the stronger the taste and healing properties will be.
4. Remove the tea sieve or strain the tea to remove the seeds.
5. Add honey or a bit of lemon to taste, if desired.
6. Enjoy the tea warm for the best stomach benefits.

Variations

- Mix anise seed with carminative herbs such as Fennel or peppermint for a better stomach aid.
- Add a cinnamon stick or a few cloves during the steeping process to improve the taste.

Storage Tips

To maintain their strength, dried anise seeds should be stored in a cool, dry place away from direct sunlight. Anise Seed Tea is best served fresh but can be kept in the refrigerator for up to 24 hours. Reheat gently before eating.

Tips for allergens

Individuals with allergies to plants in the Apiaceae family, such as celery, carrot, or parsley, should practice care when trying anise seed for the first time. Always start with a small amount to test for any bad reactions.

Gentian Root Bitters

Beneficial effects

Gentian Root Bitters are praised for their ability to boost digestion, improve gut enzyme production, and increase nutrient uptake. This traditional method can be beneficial for those suffering from heartburn, bloating, and food loss. Its bitter traits trigger the taste receptors, telling the body to release gut enzymes and bile, which supports healthy digestion.

Ingredients

- Two tablespoons dried gentian root
- 1/2 cup high-proof alcohol (such as vodka or brandy, at least 80 proof)
- 2 cups water
- Zest of 1 organic lemon
- One tablespoon of dried orange peel
- One teaspoon of dried ginger root
- One cinnamon stick
- Honey (optional, to taste)

Instructions

1. Combine the dried gentian root and high-proof alcohol in a clean, sealed jar. Ensure the gentian root is thoroughly soaked in the booze.
2. Seal the jar tightly and let it sit in a cool, dark place for two weeks, shaking it gently every few days to mix the contents.

3. After two weeks, strain the alcohol mixture, removing the gentian plant.
4. Mix water, lemon zest, dried orange peel, ginger root, and cinnamon stick in a pot. Bring to a boil, then reduce heat and cook for 20 minutes.
5. Strain the liquid into the jar holding the alcohol mixture, removing the solids.
6. If wanted, add honey to sweeten the bitters.
7. Store the bitters in a clean, sealed bottle.

Variations

- For a non-alcoholic version, replace the high-proof booze with apple cider vinegar.
- Add herbs and spices like cardamom or star anise to make a unique taste flavour.
- For a sweeter version, increase the amount of honey or add a bit of maple syrup.

Storage Tips

Store the Gentian Root Bitters in a tight jar in a cool, dark place. The bitters will keep for up to 6 months. For best taste, use within the first three months.

Tips for allergens

Individuals with allergies to any Ingredients should avoid them or find suitable replacements. For those allergic to booze, the non-alcoholic form made with apple cider vinegar gives a great choice.

HERBS FOR MANAGING STRESS AND ANXIETY

LAVENDER AND CHAMOMILE SLEEP TEA

Beneficial effects

Lavender and Chamomile Sleep Tea combines the healing properties of lavender and chamomile, making it an excellent natural treatment for lowering worry and stress and promoting a restful night's sleep. Lavender is known for its calming and relaxing benefits, while chamomile has been used for ages to help with sleepiness and to ease the mind. Together, they make a potent mix to help soothe the nervous system and improve sleep quality.

Ingredients

- One teaspoon of dried lavender flowers
- One teaspoon of dried chamomile flowers
- 8 ounces of boiling water
- Honey or lemon (optional, for taste)

Instructions

1. Place the dried lavender and chamomile flowers in a tea infuser or right into a cup.
2. Pour the hot water over the flowers, ensuring they are fully covered.
3. Cover the cup and allow the tea to steep for 5-10 minutes. The longer it steeps, the stronger the taste and healing properties will be.
4. Remove the tea sieve or strain the tea to remove the flowers.
5. Add honey or a bit of lemon to taste, if desired.
6. Enjoy the tea warm, ideally 30 minutes before bedtime, to help promote a peaceful and sound sleep.

Variations

- For a stronger taste, add a cinnamon stick or a few slices of fresh ginger to the tea while it steeps.
- Combine with a small amount of valerian root for an even better sleep aid. Note that valerian root has a robust taste.
- Let the tea cool down for a cold version and then chill for 1-2 hours. Serve over ice for a cool, calming drink.

Storage Tips

Store extra dried lavender and chamomile flowers in closed cases in a cool, dark place to keep their strength. Prepared Lavender and Chamomile Sleep Tea is best enjoyed fresh but can be kept in the refrigerator for up to 24 hours. Reheat gently before eating.

Tips for allergens

Individuals with allergies to plants in the Asteraceae family, including chamomile and lavender, should continue with care when trying this tea for the first time. Always start with a small amount to test for any bad reactions.

VALERIAN ROOT CALMING TINCTURE

Beneficial effects

Valerian Root Calming Tincture is a natural solid drug known for its ability to lower anxiety, promote relaxation, and improve sleep quality. Its relaxing qualities help calm the nervous system, making it an excellent choice for those dealing with stress and nervousness.

Ingredients

- 1 cup of dried valerian root
- 2 cups of high-proof alcohol (such as vodka or brandy, at least 80 proof)

Instructions

1. Place the dried valerian root in a clean, dry jar.
2. Pour the alcohol over the valerian root, fully covering the roots.
3. Seal the jar tightly and mark it with the date and contents.
4. Store the jar in a cool, dark place for 4 to 6 weeks, shaking it gently every few days to mix the contents.
5. After soaking, strain the liquor through a fine mesh strainer or cheesecloth into another clean jar or bottle, pressing the plant material to remove as much liquid as possible.
6. Label the end product with the date and ingredients. Store in a cool, dark place.

Variations

For those allergic to alcohol, a glycerin-based drink can be made by changing the alcohol with veggie glycerin and water. Use a ratio of 3 parts glycerin to 1 part water.

To improve the relaxing benefits, add other herbs, such as lavender or chamomile, to the tea during the soaking process.

Storage Tips

When appropriately kept in a cool, dark place, the Valerian Root Calming Tincture can last for several years. Ensure the bottle is tightly shut to prevent loss and breakdown of the active chemicals.

Tips for allergens

Valerian root is usually well-tolerated, but people with allergies to valerian or other plants in the Valerianaceae family should continue with care. Always start with a small amount to test for any bad reactions.

LEMON BALM AND PASSIONFLOWER INFUSION

Beneficial effects

Lemon Balm and Passionflower Infusion is a relaxing plant medicine known for its ability to ease signs of worry and stress. With its mild relaxing effects, Lemon balm promotes rest and a feeling of calm, while Passionflower is known for treating nervousness and sleepiness. Together, they make a potent mix to help soothe the nervous system, reduce stress, and improve sleep quality.

Ingredients

- One tablespoon of dried lemon balm leaves
- One tablespoon of dried Passionflower
- 2 cups boiling water
- Honey or lemon (optional, for taste)

Instructions

1. Place the dried lemon balm leaves and Passionflower in a tea bag or straight into a kettle.
2. Pour 2 cups of hot water over the herbs.
3. Cover and allow the herbs to steep for 10-15 minutes. This steeping time releases the herbs' healing powers into the water.
4. Strain the liquid into cups, dumping the used leaves.
5. If wanted, add honey or a bit of lemon to taste.
6. Enjoy this tea in the evening or whenever you need to relax and reduce stress.

Variations

- Add a teaspoon of dried lavender to the blend for extra calm effects.
- To improve the taste, include a cinnamon stick or a few slices of fresh ginger in the mug while steeping.

Storage Tips

It's best to make this combination fresh to ensure the maximum healing benefits. However, if needed, you can store any extra injection in the refrigerator for up to 24 hours. Reheat gently before drinking, but do not cook to preserve the healing ingredients of the herbs.

Tips for allergens

Individuals with allergies to plants in the Lamiaceae family, including lemon balm and Passionflower, should continue cautiously and visit a healthcare source before trying this tea.

Beneficial effects

Holy Basil (Tulsi) Stress Relief Tea is famous for its adaptogenic traits, which help the body fight stress and support mental health. It is known to lower cortisol levels, improve energy, and help the immune system. Additionally, Tulsi has anti-anxiety and calming qualities, making it an excellent plant for controlling worry and anxiety.

Ingredients

- 1-2 teaspoons of dried Holy Basil (Tulsi) leaves
- 8 ounces of boiling water
- Honey or lemon (optional, for taste)

Instructions

1. Place the dried Holy Basil leaves in a tea bag or cup.
2. Pour the hot water over the leaves and cover the cup to prevent burning oils from escaping.
3. Allow the tea to steep for 5-7 minutes, based on the needed strength.
4. Remove the tea sieve or strain the tea to remove the leaves.
5. Add honey or a bit of lemon to taste, if desired.
6. Enjoy the tea warm, best in the morning or evening, to help soothe stress and worry.

Variations

- For a cooling effect in the summer, chill the tea and serve with a slice of lemon.
- Combine with chamomile or lavender for better relaxing effects.
- Add a pinch of ground cinnamon or ginger for a warming, spicy twist.

Storage Tips

Store dried Holy Basil leaves in a covered jar in a cool, dark place to keep their usefulness. The tea can be chilled for up to 24 hours. Reheat slowly without cooking, or enjoy cold.

Tips for allergens

Individuals with allergies to plants in the Lamiaceae family (such as mint, oregano, and lavender) should continue with care when trying Holy Basil for the first time. Always start with a small amount to test for any bad reactions.

ASHWAGANDHA AND RHODIOLA ADAPTOGEN ELIXIR

Beneficial effects

The Ashwagandha and Rhodiola Adaptogen Elixir mixes the stress-relieving traits of Ashwagandha with Rhodiola's uplifting and mood-enhancing benefits. This potent mix supports the body's response to stress, improves mental clarity and focus, and boosts general energy levels. Ashwagandha, known for its ability to lower cortisol levels, works perfectly with Rhodiola, which helps fight tiredness and sadness, making this elixir an excellent choice for handling stress and anxiety.

Ingredients

- One teaspoon of Ashwagandha powder
- One teaspoon of Rhodiola powder
- 1 cup of water
- Honey or maple syrup (optional, to taste)

Instructions

1. Bring 1 cup of water to a boil in a small pot.
2. Reduce the heat to low and add the Ashwagandha and Rhodiola powders, stirring well to mix.
3. Simmer the mixture for 10 minutes, allowing the herbs to taste the water.
4. Remove from heat and strain the mixture into a cup, removing the extra herb powder.
5. If wanted, add honey or maple syrup to sweeten the juice.
6. Enjoy the beverage warm, which is best in the morning to start your day or during moments of stress to help calm the mind and body.

Variations

For an extra boost, include a slice of fresh ginger or a pinch of cinnamon during the cooking process for their added antioxidant and anti-inflammatory effects.

This drink can also be mixed with a cup of warm milk (dairy or plant-based) instead of water for a creamier, more soothing beverage.

Storage Tips

To ensure maximum strength and efficiency, it's best to make the Ashwagandha and Rhodiola Adaptogen Elixir fresh for each use. However, if you need to store it, keep the drink in a sealed jar in the refrigerator for up to 24 hours. Reheat gently before eating.

Tips for allergens

Individuals with specific plant problems should visit a healthcare source before taking Ashwagandha or Rhodiola. Both plants are usually well-tolerated, but it's important to start with a small amount to watch for any bad reactions.

VALERIAN: OVERVIEW AND BENEFITS

Valerian, officially known as Valeriana officinalis, is an annual ornamental plant native to Europe and parts of Asia. It has since been naturalized in North America. The plant is known for its sweetly scented pink or white flowers and the strong, distinct smell of its roots used in herbal treatment. Valerian grows in fields and woods, growing in damp situations. It reaches a height of up to 5 feet, having complex leaves and groups of small, umbrella-like flowers. The use of valerian goes back thousands of years, with a rich history of medicine use described by old Greeks and Romans. Hippocrates, the father of medicine, described its healing benefits, and Galen later suggested it as a cure for sleepiness. This past use has carried into current times, where valerian root is widely known for its grounding and relaxing benefits.

Valerian's effects are mainly linked to its volatile oils, iridoids, valeric acid, and other substances such as isovaleric acid and a range of vitamins. These chemicals interact with the gamma-aminobutyric acid (GABA) receptor, a protein responsible for controlling nerve impulses in your brain and nervous system. By stopping the breakdown of GABA, valerian root can lower feelings of anxiety and promote calmness, making it an effective natural medicine for people suffering from nervous stress, anxiety, and sleepiness. Clinical studies have backed the use of valerian for improving sleep quality without the hangover effect linked with some sleep drugs. It is often mixed with calming herbs, such as lemon balm, hops, and chamomile, to improve its sleep-promoting benefits. Valerian is available in various forms, including pills, drinks, and teas, allowing for freedom to work into an evening practice to support restful sleep. Beyond its relaxing qualities, valerian has been studied for its ability to ease menstrual cramps and muscle stress. The antispasmodic action of valerenic acid can help to soothe muscle cramps and stomach pain, making it a flexible plant for treating a range of conditions linked to tension and stress. When using valerian, starting with a low amount is essential to measure tolerance and gradually raise it as needed. While valerian is generally considered safe for most adults, it's advisable to consult with a healthcare provider before starting any new supplement, especially for those with existing health conditions, pregnant or breastfeeding women, or individuals taking medications, as valerian can interact with certain drugs. Incorporating valerian into one's health practice offers a natural, effective way to reduce stress, worry, and sleep problems. Its long history of use, mixed with current scientific study, underlines the worth of valerian as an essential herb in the practice of herbal medicine for supporting rest and well-being.

EXPLORING PASSIONFLOWER: USES & BENEFITS

Passionflower, officially known as Passiflora incarnata, is an annual growing plant famous for its beautiful flowers and healing powers. Native to the southeastern United States, this plant has been utilized for ages by Native American groups for its healing benefits. The delicate, purple and white flowers give way to a tasty fruit, yet the leaves and stems are gathered for health benefits. Passionflower includes several active substances, including flavonoids and alkaloids, which are thought to add to its calming and relaxing benefits. These chemicals work jointly to raise gamma-aminobutyric acid (GABA) in the brain, a neurotransmitter that helps manage mood and support sleep. This mode of action makes Passionflower a popular natural treatment for anxiety, stress, and sleeplessness, giving a gentle option to drug sedatives. Beyond its use for nervous system support, Passionflower has been widely used to ease signs of stomach upset linked to anxiety, such as nervous indigestion and cramps. Its antispasmodic benefits help relax the smooth muscles of the stomach, relieving pain and improving gut health. Passionflower can be a drink, syrup, or pill for those looking for natural ways to control stress and improve sleep. Its mild calming effect makes it suitable for evening use, promoting peaceful sleep without the grogginess often associated with drug sleep aids. When adding PassionflowerPassionflower into a fitness practice, it's essential to start with a low amount to measure individual tolerance and speak with a healthcare provider, especially for those taking other drugs or with underlying health problems. In herbal medicine, Passionflower shows the power of plants to support the body's natural mending processes, giving a time-tested answer for modern-day stress and sleep problems.

LAVENDER AND MELATONIN: NATURAL SLEEP BENEFITS

Lavender, or Lavandula, is a group of flowering plants in the mint family. Renowned for its calming aroma, lavender is a staple in the fragrance and makeup business and holds a respected spot in plant medicine. Its flowers and essential oils are used for their calming, relaxing, and anti-inflammatory qualities, making lavender a go-to plant for promoting ease and improving sleep quality. By enhancing the activity of hormones that control mood and sleep, lavender oil can be spread in the bedroom to create a quiet environment suitable for easy sleep or applied directly in weakened form for a calming effect. Natural melatonin sources, such as cherry juice, especially from tart cherries, offer a healthy way to improve sleep. Melatonin, a hormone that controls the sleep-wake cycle, is found in certain foods, with sour cherries being among the best sources. Consuming tart cherry juice has been shown to boost melatonin levels in the body, improving sleep time and quality. This natural method is especially beneficial for individuals facing jet lag or irregular sleep habits, giving a safe and effective way to fix the body's internal clock. Incorporating lavender and natural melatonin sources like cherry juice into the evening routine can help improve sleep quality. Whether sipping on a glass of tart cherry juice an hour before bed or smelling lavender oil in the bedroom, these old treatments offer a balanced and straightforward approach to achieving restorative sleep, reflecting the timeless wisdom of plant medicine in supporting modern well-being.

HOPS: NAME, DESCRIPTION, AND BENEFITS OF HOPS.

Hops, officially known as Humulus lupulus, are biennial plants known for their use in making beer, but their benefits stretch far beyond as a brewing element. Native to Europe, Western Asia, and North America, hops have been grown for their healing benefits for ages. The plant features cone-shaped flowers, the central part of which is used in brewing and herbal medicine. These green cones, or strobiles, contain chemicals such as humulone and lupulone, which add to hops' distinctive bitter taste and are also charged with different health benefits. Traditionally, hops have been used to treat a range of ailments, from changes in sleep to nervousness and restlessness. The calming benefits of hops are well-documented, making them a popular natural treatment for sleepiness and other sleep problems. This relaxed effect is linked to the substance methyl butanol, which is found in hops and has been shown to have calming properties. Hops can be used in drinks, drugs, and even pillows filled with dried hops to promote relaxation and improve sleep quality.

In addition to their relaxing effects, hops have been studied for their potential to ease signs of menopause, such as hot flashes and mood swings. The phytoestrogens in hops may help balance hormone levels, reducing menopause symptoms. Moreover, hops show anti-inflammatory and antibacterial properties, making them helpful in treating skin problems and improving general skin health. They have also been studied for their antioxidant content, which can help remove free radicals and lower oxidative stress in the body. While hops are usually considered safe for most people, it is essential to speak with a healthcare provider before adding them to your exercise routine, especially for those with hormone-sensitive conditions or those taking calming drugs. Hops offers a natural, balanced approach to healing sleep problems, hormonal changes, and inflammatory conditions, following the principles of herbal medicine by tapping the power of plants to support health and well-being.

LEMON BALM: OVERVIEW AND BENEFITS

Lemon Balm, officially called Melissa officinalis, is an annual mint family tree known for its lemon-scented leaves. It comes from southern Europe and the Mediterranean and has been widely grown abroad. Recognizable by its tiny white flowers and deeply twisted leaves, lemon balm is prized for its healing qualities and broad use in traditional and modern plant medicine. The herb's benefits are numerous due mainly to its rich content of volatile oils, tannins, flavonoids, and terpenes, which collectively add to its calming, antiviral, and antibiotic qualities. Historically, lemon balm has improved happiness and brain function, lowered fear and stress, and promoted sleep. Its success in relaxing the nervous system makes it a popular choice for those seeking natural treatments for anxiousness and sleepiness.

Additionally, lemon balm has been used to help digestion, ease menstrual cramps, and treat cold sores due to its medical effects against the herpes simplex virus. Incorporating lemon balm into one's exercise routine can be as easy as making tea from its fresh or dried leaves, which not only uses its health benefits but also offers peace. The herb can also be applied straight in balms and creams for skin irritations and cold sore care, showing flexibility. Despite its gentle nature, speaking with a healthcare provider before adding lemon balm to your diet is advised to avoid possible clashes, especially for those on medicine. Lemon balm stands out in the herbal world for its wonderful smell and gentle yet powerful healing qualities, reflecting the spirit of herbal medicine's power to balance body and mind. Its ease of growing and wide range of uses make it a valuable addition to any plant yard or natural health tool, carrying the tradition of old drugs in modern wellness practices.

DIGESTION'S ROLE IN STRESS RELIEF

The complex link between digestion and worry, often called the gut-brain axis, underscores the profound effect that stomach health can have on mental well-being and vice versa. This relationship is based on the complex signalling network that links the gut system with the brain, stressing the importance of supporting stomach health to control stress and worry. Herbs, with their various healing qualities, offer a natural and effective way to improve gut function, thereby adding to better stress control and general mental health. Peppermint, officially known as Mentha piperita, stands out for its antispasmodic traits, which can ease stomach pain by relaxing the smooth muscles of the digestive system. This helps reduce symptoms such as bloating and cramps and mitigates the physical signs of stress within the digestive system. Incorporating peppermint into one's diet, whether as a calm tea or a colouring agent, can thus serve as a simple yet powerful means of supporting physical and mental health. Ginger, another old plant with a long history of use in traditional medicine, causes a warming and exciting effect on the digestive system. Its anti-inflammatory and carminative actions can soothe the stomach walls and improve gastric movement, allowing the efficient processing and removal of food. By improving stomach function, ginger helps ensure that the physical pain associated with poor eating does not raise fear and anxiety.

Moreover, its exciting taste and smell can boost the mood, giving a physical means of stress release. Chamomile, known for its calming benefits, is also helpful for gut health. Its antispasmodic and anti-inflammatory effects can soothe swollen mucous membranes in the digestive system, easing symptoms of indigestion and gastritis that may appear in response to stress. By promoting resting and relieving stomach pain, chamomile tea can serve as a gentle and effective cure for anxiety and digestive problems, reflecting the general approach of plant medicine. With its unique liquorice-like taste, Fennel is another vegetable that can be particularly helpful for those dealing with stress-related stomach problems. Its carminative traits help to clear gas and ease bloating, while its antispasmodic action can reduce cramps and discomfort in the digestive system. Fennel seeds can be eaten after meals to help digestion or made into tea to enjoy their soothing effects on the gut and the mind. Incorporating these plants into one's daily routine can be a simple yet effective way to support gut health and, by extension, handle stress and anxiety. Whether by making and enjoying herbal drinks or adding these herbs to meals and snacks, people can tap the power of herbal medicine to support their digestive system and improve their resistance to stress. This combined method not only treats the physical parts of digestion but also respects the strong effect of mental well-being on general health, giving a complete plan for improving the quality of life in the modern world.

TEN HERBAL REMEDIES FOR MANAGING STRESS AND ANXIETY

Lavender and Chamomile Sleep Tea

Beneficial effects

Lavender and Chamomile Sleep Tea combines the healing properties of lavender and chamomile, making it an excellent natural treatment for lowering worry and stress and promoting a restful night's sleep. Lavender is known for its calming and relaxing benefits, while chamomile has been used for ages to help with sleepiness and to ease the mind. Together, they make a solid mix to help soothe the nervous system and improve sleep quality.

Ingredients

- One teaspoon of dried lavender flowers
- One teaspoon of dried chamomile flowers
- 8 ounces of boiling water
- Honey or lemon (optional, for taste)

Instructions

1. Place the dried lavender and chamomile flowers in a tea infuser or right into a cup.
2. Pour the hot water over the flowers, ensuring they are fully covered.
3. Cover the cup and allow the tea to steep for 5-10 minutes. The longer it steeps, the stronger the taste and healing properties will be.
4. Remove the tea sieve or strain the tea to remove the flowers.
5. Add honey or a bit of lemon to taste, if desired.
6. Enjoy the tea warm, ideally 30 minutes before bedtime, to help promote a peaceful and sound sleep.

Variations

- For a stronger taste, add a cinnamon stick or a few slices of fresh ginger to the tea while it steeps.
- Combine with a small amount of valerian root for an even better sleep aid. Note that valerian root has an extreme taste.
- Let the tea cool down for a cold version and then chill for 1-2 hours. Serve over ice for a cool, calming drink.

Storage Tips

Store extra dried lavender and chamomile flowers in closed cases in a cool, dark place to keep their strength. Prepared Lavender and Chamomile Sleep Tea is best enjoyed fresh but can be kept in the refrigerator for up to 24 hours. Reheat gently before eating.

Tips for allergens

Individuals with allergies to plants in the Asteraceae family, including chamomile and lavender, should continue with care when trying this tea for the first time. Always start with a small amount to test for any bad reactions.

Valerian Root Calming Tincture

Beneficial effects

Valerian Root relaxing Tincture is famous for its relaxing qualities, making it an essential friend against insomnia, worry, and stress. By improving GABA (gamma-aminobutyric acid) levels in the brain, valerian root promotes calm and allows a deeper, more refreshing sleep. This natural treatment is particularly beneficial for individuals wanting a non-habit-forming choice of pharmaceutical sleep aids and anxiolytics.

Ingredients

- 1 cup of dried valerian root
- 2 cups of vodka or another high-proof alcohol

Instructions

1. Place the dried valerian root into a clean, dry glass jar.
2. Pour the vodka over the roots, ensuring they are completely covered. Add more booze until the valerian root is covered by at least an inch of liquid.
3. Seal the jar tightly and shake it to ensure the valerian root is thoroughly soaked with the alcohol.
4. Label the jar with the current date and contents. Store the jar in a cool, dark place for 4 to 6 weeks, shaking it daily to help the extraction process.
5. After soaking, strain the booze through a fine mesh strainer or cheesecloth into a clean, dark glass bottle. Squeeze or press the wet valerian root to remove as much juice as possible.
6. Discard the used valerian root. Label the bottle with the date and contents.

Variations

- For a non-alcoholic version, replace the vodka with apple cider vinegar or glycerin, changing the steeping time as needed. Note that the strength and shelf life may vary with these replacements.
- Enhance the relaxing benefits by adding other herbs, such as lavender or chamomile, to the drink. An average amount is three parts valerian root to 1 part of the extra plant.

Storage Tips

Store the Valerian Root Calming Tincture in a cool, dark place. When appropriately kept, the juice can stay vital for up to five years. Ensure the bottle is tightly shut to prevent loss and breakdown of the active chemicals.

Tips for allergens

Individuals with allergies to valerian or other plants in the Valerianaceae family should avoid this drink. As with any natural medicine, it's suggested to speak with a healthcare provider before use, especially for those with medical problems or those taking drugs, to avoid possible conflicts.

Lemon Balm and Passionflower Infusion

Beneficial effects

Lemon Balm and Passionflower Infusion is a gentle yet effective natural cure for easing worry and stress and promoting a peaceful state of mind. With its cooling benefits, Lemon balm helps to reduce fear and anxiety, while Passionflower is known for improving sleep quality and soothing nervous energy. Together, they make a compelling mix that can help relax the body and mind, making it easier to unwind after a busy day and achieve a restful night's sleep.

Ingredients

- One tablespoon of dried lemon balm leaves
- One tablespoon of dried Passionflower
- 2 cups boiling water
- Honey or lemon (optional, for taste)

Instructions

1. Place the dried lemon balm leaves and Passionflower in a tea bag or straight into a kettle.
2. Pour 2 cups of hot water over the herbs.
3. Cover and allow the herbs to steep for 10-15 minutes. This steeping time releases the herbs' healing powers into the water.
4. Strain the liquid into cups, dumping the used leaves.
5. If wanted, add honey or a bit of lemon to taste.
6. Enjoy this tea in the evening or whenever you need to relax and reduce stress.

Variations

- Add a teaspoon of dried lavender to the blend for extra calm effects.
- To improve the taste, include a cinnamon stick or a few slices of fresh ginger in the mug while steeping.

Storage Tips

It's best to make this combination fresh to ensure the maximum healing benefits. However, if needed, you can store any extra injection in the refrigerator for up to 24 hours. Reheat gently before drinking, but do not cook to preserve the healing ingredients of the herbs.

Tips for allergens

Individuals with allergies to plants in the Lamiaceae family, including lemon balm and Passionflower, should continue cautiously and visit a healthcare source before trying this tea.

Holy Basil (Tulsi) Stress Relief Tea

Beneficial effects

Holy Basil (Tulsi) Stress Relief Tea is famous for its adaptogenic traits, which help the body fight stress and support mental health. It is known to lower cortisol levels, improve energy, and help the immune system. Additionally, Tulsi has anti-anxiety and calming qualities, making it an excellent plant for controlling worry and anxiety.

Ingredients

- 1-2 teaspoons of dried Holy Basil (Tulsi) leaves
- 8 ounces of boiling water
- Honey or lemon (optional, for taste)

Instructions

1. Place the dried Holy Basil leaves in a tea bag or cup.
2. Pour the hot water over the leaves and cover the cup to prevent burning oils from escaping.
3. Allow the tea to steep for 5-7 minutes, based on the needed strength.
4. Remove the tea sieve or strain the tea to remove the leaves.
5. Add honey or a bit of lemon to taste, if desired.
6. Enjoy the tea warm, best in the morning or evening, to help soothe stress and worry.

Variations

- For a cooling effect in the summer, chill the tea and serve with a slice of lemon.
- Combine with chamomile or lavender for better relaxing effects.
- Add a pinch of ground cinnamon or ginger for a warming, spicy twist.

Storage Tips

Store dried Holy Basil leaves in a covered jar in a cool, dark place to keep their usefulness. The tea can be chilled for up to 24 hours. Reheat slowly without cooking, or enjoy cold.

Tips for allergens

Individuals with allergies to plants in the Lamiaceae family (such as mint, oregano, and lavender) should continue with care when trying Holy Basil for the first time. Always start with a small amount to test for any bad reactions.

Ashwagandha and Rhodiola Adaptogen Elixir
Beneficial effects

The Ashwagandha and Rhodiola Adaptogen Elixir is a potent mix that fights stress, improves mental focus, and boosts energy. Ashwagandha is known for its ability to lower cortisol levels and combat the effects of stress, while Rhodiola is celebrated for its fatigue-fighting and mood-enhancing qualities. Together, they form a potent mixture that supports the body's natural response to pressures, improves brain function, and promotes general well-being.

Ingredients

- One teaspoon of Ashwagandha powder
- One teaspoon of Rhodiola powder
- 1 cup of water
- Honey or maple syrup (optional, to taste)

Instructions

1. Bring 1 cup of water to a boil in a small pot.
2. Reduce the heat to low and add the Ashwagandha and Rhodiola powders, stirring well to ensure they dissolve fully.
3. Simmer the mixture for 10 minutes, allowing the herbs to taste the water.
4. Remove from heat and strain the mixture into a cup, removing the extra herb powder.
5. If wanted, sweeten with honey or maple syrup to taste.
6. Enjoy the beverage warm, best in the morning or early afternoon, to harness its stress-relieving and energy-boosting benefits.

Variations

- Introduce a slice of fresh ginger or a pinch of turmeric during the cooking process for an extra health boost.
- This drink can also be mixed with a cup of warm milk (dairy or plant-based) instead of water for a creamier, more soothing beverage.

Storage Tips

It's best to make the Ashwagandha and Rhodiola Adaptogen Elixir fresh for each use to improve its strength and value. However, if you need to store it, keep the drink in a sealed jar in the refrigerator for up to 24 hours. Reheat gently before eating.

Tips for allergens

Individuals with specific plant problems should visit a healthcare source before taking Ashwagandha or Rhodiola. Both plants are usually well-tolerated, but it's important to start with a small amount to watch for any bad reactions.

Skullcap and Hops Relaxation Tincture

Beneficial effects

The Skullcap and Hops Relaxation Tincture combines the relaxing and nerve-soothing properties of skullcap with the hypnotic qualities of hops, making a solid fix for anxiety, stress, and sleep problems. Skullcap is known for its ability to ease nerve stress and support mental well-being, while hops add to better sleep quality and rest. Together, they make a compelling mix that can help calm a busy mind and promote a peaceful state, making it easier to rest and fall asleep.

Ingredients

- 1/4 cup dried skullcap herb
- 1/4 cup dried hops flowers
- 1 pint of high-proof alcohol (such as vodka or brandy, at least 80 proof)

Instructions

1. Combine the dried skullcap and hops flowers in a clean, dry jar.
2. Pour the high-proof alcohol over the herbs, ensuring they are fully covered.
3. Seal the jar tightly and mark it with the date and contents.
4. Store the jar in a cool, dark place for 4 to 6 weeks, shaking it gently every few days to mix the contents and promote extraction.
5. After soaking, strain the liquor through a fine mesh strainer or cheesecloth into another clean jar or bottle, pressing the plant material to remove as much liquid as possible.
6. Label the end product with the date and ingredients. Store in a cool, dark place.

Variations

- For those allergic to alcohol, a glycerin-based drink can be made by changing the alcohol with a mixture of veggie glycerin and water. Use a ratio of 3 parts glycerin to 1 part water.
- To improve the calm benefits, add a teaspoon of dried lavender or chamomile to the liquor during the boiling process.

Storage Tips

When appropriately kept in a cool, dark place, the Skullcap and Hops Relaxation Tincture lasts several years. Ensure the bottle is tightly shut to prevent loss and breakdown of the active chemicals.

Tips for allergens

Individuals with reactions to plants in the Lamiaceae family (such as skullcap) or to hops should continue carefully and visit a healthcare source before using this medicine. Always start with a small amount to test for any bad reactions.

Kava Kava Stress Relief Drink

Beneficial effects

Kava Kava Stress Relief Drink is famous for its peaceful qualities, significantly easing worry and stress. Kava, a herb native to the Pacific Islands, has been used for ages in traditional drinks for its calming benefits. It works on the nerve system to promote rest without changing brain function, making it an excellent choice for those looking to naturally lower stress and worry levels.

Ingredients

- Two tablespoons of ground Kava Kava root
- 8 ounces of warm water (not boiling, to preserve the kavalactones)
- Honey or maple syrup (optional, to taste)
- A pinch of cinnamon (optional for flavour)

Instructions

1. Place the ground Kava Kava root into a fine mesh strainer or cheesecloth.
2. Hold the sieve or cheesecloth over a bowl and pour the warm water over the Kava Kava root.
3. Allow the mixture to sit for 10-15 minutes, occasionally squeezing the sieve or cheesecloth to remove the liquid thoroughly.
4. Once the juice has been fully taken, trash the ground root.
5. Transfer the Kava Kava drink into a cup. If wanted, sweeten with honey or maple syrup and add a pinch of cinnamon for taste.
6. Stir well before drinking.

Variations

- For a more excellent beverage, leave the Kava Kava drink to chill in the refrigerator for an hour before serving over ice.
- Blend the finished drink with coconut milk for a creamier texture and tropical taste.
- Add a slice of lemon or lime for a refreshing citrus note.

Storage Tips

Kava Kava Stress Relief Drink is best enjoyed fresh. However, if necessary, it can be saved in the refrigerator for up to 24 hours. Stir well before drinking if separation happens.

Tips for allergens

Individuals with a history of liver problems should speak with a healthcare provider before taking Kava Kava, as it has been linked with liver damage in rare cases. Always start with a small amount to ensure patience and avoid bad reactions.

Passionflower and Lemon Balm Tea

Beneficial effects

Passionflower and Lemon Balm Tea is a gentle, natural medicine that reduces signs of fear and anxiety. This plant mix combines the calming qualities of lemon balm with the relaxing effects of Passionflower, making it an ideal drink for boosting rest and improving sleep quality. Passionflower is known for boosting gamma-aminobutyric acid (GABA) in the brain, which helps lower brain activity and may improve mood and reduce stress. Lemon balm helps this by adding to higher GABA levels and giving mood-enhancing and stress-relieving properties.

Ingredients

- One teaspoon of dried Passionflower
- One teaspoon of dried lemon balm leaves
- 8 ounces of boiling water
- Honey or lemon slice (optional, for taste)

Instructions

1. Place the dried Passionflower and lemon balm leaves in a tea bag or right into a cup.
2. Pour the hot water over the herbs, ensuring they are fully covered.
3. Cover the cup and allow the herbs to steep for 10-15 minutes. This causes the herbs' healing powers to be released entirely into the water.
4. Remove the tea strainer or strain the tea to remove the extra herbs.
5. Add honey or a bit of lemon to improve the taste if desired.
6. Enjoy this tea in the evening or whenever you need to rest and reduce stress.

Variations

- Add a small amount of valerian root to the tea mix for a better cooling effect. Note that valerian root has a robust taste.
- Add a cinnamon stick or a few slices of fresh ginger to the cup while steeping to make a more complex taste profile.
- Allow the tea to cool and chill for those wanting a cold brew. Serve over ice for a cool, calming drink.

Storage Tips

Preparing Passionflower and Lemon Balm Tea fresh for each use is best to ensure the maximum healing benefits. However, if you need to store it, keep the tea in a sealed jar in the refrigerator for up to 24 hours. Reheat gently before eating, or enjoy it cold.

Tips for allergens

Individuals with allergies to plants in the Passifloraceae family (such as Passionflower) or the Lamiaceae family (such as lemon balm) should continue carefully and visit a healthcare source before trying this tea. Always start with a small amount to test for any bad reactions.

Chamomile and Lavender Bath Soak

Beneficial effects

The Chamomile and Lavender Bath Soak combines the calming properties of chamomile with the relaxing effects of lavender, creating a healing bath that eases stress, lowers anxiety, and promotes a restful night's sleep. Chamomile is known for its ability to soothe the mind and body. At the same time, lavender's natural taste has been linked with dropping blood pressure and heart rate, further improving relaxation and stress release.

Ingredients

- 1/2 cup dried chamomile flowers
- 1/2 cup dried lavender buds
- 2 cups Epsom salt
- Optional: A few drops of lavender essential oil for enhanced aromatic benefits

Instructions

1. Mix the dried chamomile leaves, dried lavender buds, and Epsom salt in a big bowl until well mixed.
2. Add a few drops of lavender essential oil to the liquid and stir thoroughly to spread the oil widely.
3. Transfer the bath soak mixture to a sealed jar for storage.
4. Add 1 cup of the bath soak mixture to warm running bath water.
5. Stir the water with your hand to help break down the Epsom salt and release the smells of the chamomile and lavender.
6. Soak in the bath for at least 20 minutes to enjoy the healing benefits.

Variations

- Add 1/4 cup of powdered milk or coconut milk powder to the drink for a hydrating soak.
- Incorporate a handful of dried rose petals for an extra flower taste and a touch of luxury.
- Add a few tablespoons of baking soda to the mixture to smooth the water and soothe the skin for extra relaxation.

Storage Tips

Store the Chamomile and Lavender Bath Soak in a tight jar in a cool, dry place to protect its strength and taste. Properly stored, the bath soak can last for up to 6 months.

Tips for allergens

Individuals with allergies to chamomile, lavender, or other plants in the Asteraceae family should practice care and may need to test for allergic reactions before thoroughly soaking in a bath. As a choice, try using careful options or removing these Ingredients altogether.

Lemon Balm and Valerian Root Sleep Aid

Beneficial effects

Lemon Balm and Valerian Root Sleep Aid is a natural medicine that promotes ease and improves sleep quality. With its calm effects, lemon balm helps reduce nervousness and create peace, while valerian root works as a tranquillizer, enhancing the ease of going to sleep and increasing sleep depth. Together, they form a potent mixture for those suffering from insomnia or restless nights, giving a gentle option to pharmaceutical sleep aids.

Ingredients

- Two tablespoons dried lemon balm leaves
- One tablespoon of dried valerian root
- 8 ounces of boiling water
- Honey or lemon (optional, for taste)

Instructions

1. Combine the dried lemon balm leaves and valerian root in a tea maker or teapot.
2. Pour the hot water over the leaves and cover to prevent the escape of burning oils.
3. Allow the mixture to sit for 10-15 minutes. The longer it steeps, the more powerful the effects.
4. Strain the mixture into a cup, removing the leaves.
5. Add honey or a bit of lemon to improve the taste if desired.
6. Drink this sleep aid about 30 minutes before bedtime to help ensure a good night's sleep.

Variations

- For those who prefer a cold beverage, this mix can be chilled in the refrigerator and enjoyed as an iced tea.
- Adding a cinnamon stick or a few slices of fresh ginger to the mixture while it steeps can provide extra taste and possible stomach benefits.
- Mix with a small amount of chamomile tea for a more powerful sleep-inducing effect.

Storage Tips

The dried lemon balm leaves and valerian root should be kept in sealed containers in a cool, dark place to keep their usefulness. The made mixture is best eaten fresh but can be kept in the refrigerator for up to 24 hours. Reheat slowly without cooking, or enjoy cold.

Tips for allergens

Individuals with responses to plants in the mint family (such as lemon balm) or valerian should continue carefully. They may want to speak with a healthcare source before trying this treatment. Maple syrup can serve as an alternative sugar for those allergic to honey.

ELDERFLOWER TEA

Beneficial effects

Elderflower Tea is a traditional medicine known for its antibiotic and immune-boosting qualities, making it an excellent choice for treating colds and flu. It helps lessen signs such as fever, phlegm, and sore throat. Elderflower also has diaphoretic benefits, meaning it can boost sweating and help lower heat naturally.

Ingredients

- Two tablespoons dried elderflowers
- 8 ounces of boiling water
- Honey or lemon (optional, for taste)

Instructions

1. Place the dried elderflowers in a tea bag or right into a cup.
2. Pour the hot water over the elderflowers.
3. Cover the cup and let it sit for 10-15 minutes. This steeping time helps the elderflowers release their healing benefits.
4. Remove the tea strainer or strain the tea to remove the elderflowers.
5. If desired, add honey or a slice of lemon to improve the taste and provide extra vitamin C.
6. Drink the tea warm, ideally 2-3 times daily, to improve its soothing effects during a cold or flu.

Variations

- Add a piece of fresh ginger or a cinnamon stick to the cup while steeping for an extra health boost.
- Combine with peppermint leaves for a soothing, more tasty blend to help clear congestion.

Storage

Tips

 Dried elderflowers should be stored in a tight jar in a cool, dark place to keep their strength. Prepared Elderflower Tea is best served fresh but can be kept in the refrigerator for up to 24 hours. Reheat gently before eating.

Tips for allergens

Individuals with allergies to plants in the Sambucus family should avoid elderflower. Honey can be removed for those with allergies or veggie tastes; maple syrup can be a plant-based sugar replacement.

YARROW AND PEPPERMINT INFUSION

Beneficial effects

Yarrow and Peppermint Infusion is a time-tested medicine known for its ability to ease signs of colds and flu. With its anti-inflammatory and cleaning benefits, Yarrow helps lower heat and supports the body's natural defences. Peppermint, on the other hand, is praised for its menthol content, which works as a natural booster, easing coughs and soothing sore throats. Together, they form a strong team that can help reduce common cold symptoms, promote relaxation, and aid in a more restful sleep during healing.

Ingredients

- One tablespoon of dried yarrow flowers
- One tablespoon of dried peppermint leaves
- 8 ounces of boiling water
- Honey or lemon (optional, for taste)

Instructions

1. Place the dried yarrow flowers and peppermint leaves in a tea bag or straight into a cup.
2. Pour the hot water over the herbs, ensuring they are fully covered.
3. Cover the cup and allow the herbs to steep for 10-15 minutes. This causes the herbs' healing powers to be released entirely into the water.
4. Remove the tea strainer or strain the tea to remove the extra herbs.
5. Add honey or a bit of lemon to improve the taste if desired.
6. Enjoy this tea warm, ideally 2-3 times daily, to help handle cold and flu symptoms.

Variations

- For an extra health boost, add a slice of fresh ginger or a pinch of cayenne pepper to the mixture while it steeps.
- Combine with elderflower for better lung benefits.
- Allow the tea to cool and chill for those wanting a cold brew. Serve over ice for a cool, healing drink.

Storage Tips

It's best to make this blend fresh for each use to ensure the most remarkable healing benefits. However, if you need to store it, keep the tea in a sealed jar in the refrigerator for up to 24 hours. Reheat gently before eating, or enjoy it cold.

Tips for allergens

Individuals with allergies to plants in the Asteraceae family, including Yarrow or peppermint, should continue carefully and contact a healthcare source before trying this mixture. Always start with a small amount to test for any bad reactions.

EUCALYPTUS STEAM INHALATION

Beneficial effects

Eucalyptus Steam Inhalation is a time-tested method for easing the symptoms of colds and flu, including congestion, cough, and lungs. The eucalyptus plant includes cineole, a solid antibiotic with calming qualities that help clear the nose tract and reduce inflammation. This natural treatment can quickly relieve nose congestion, increase sinus flow, and improve breathing.

Ingredients

- 3 to 4 cups of boiling water
- Two teaspoons of dried eucalyptus leaves or 5-10 drops of essential oil.

Instructions

1. Boil 3 to 4 cups of water and pour it into a big heatproof bowl.
2. Add two teaspoons of dried eucalyptus leaves or 5-10 drops of essential oil to the hot water.
3. Lean over the bowl, keeping a safe distance to avoid burns, and cover your head and the bowl with a big towel to catch the steam.
4. Inhale the steam deeply for 5-10 minutes, taking breaks as needed. Close your eyes to avoid pain.
5. Repeat 2-3 times daily for relief from phlegm and cough.

Variations

- For extra antibiotic and healing effects, add a teaspoon of dried thyme or a few drops of tea tree oil to the water.
- Incorporate a tablespoon of sea salt into the hot water to improve the cooling effect.

Storage Tips

If using dried eucalyptus leaves, keep them in a covered jar in a cool, dark place to protect their usefulness. Eucalyptus essential oil should be kept in a dark glass bottle away from direct sunlight.

Tips for allergens

Individuals with asthma or allergies to eucalyptus should continue with caution and may want to speak with a healthcare source before trying this treatment. If using essential oils, ensure they are medical grade and safe for breathing.

PINE NEEDLE TEA

Beneficial effects

Pine Needle Tea is famous for its high vitamin C content and ability to support lung health, making it an excellent treatment for colds and flu. The tea is known for its antioxidant qualities, which can help beat illnesses and improve the immune system. Pine needle tea has also been widely used to ease phlegm and soothe sore throats.

Ingredients

- One tablespoon of fresh pine needles (preferably from white pine, ensuring they are free from pesticides and not from a toxic variety)

- 8 ounces of boiling water
- Honey or lemon (optional, for taste)

Instructions

1. Carefully wash the pine leaves to clear any dirt or trash.
2. Chop the pine leaves finely to improve the surface area for soaking.
3. Place the chopped pine needles in a cup or a tea strainer.
4. Pour 8 ounces of hot water over the pine leaves.
5. Cover and steep for 10-15 minutes. The longer it steeps, the stronger the taste and healing properties will be.
6. Strain the tea to remove the pine seeds.
7. Add honey or a bit of lemon to taste, if desired.
8. Enjoy the tea warm, ideally 2-3 times a day during cold and flu season, for the best benefits.

Variations

- Add a slice of fresh ginger or a dash of cinnamon while steeping for extra lung support.
- Combine with elderberry juice for an extra health boost.
- For a more refreshing version, chill the tea and serve with a slice of lemon.

Storage Tips

Fresh pine needles should be used quickly but kept in the refrigerator for up to a week. Pine Needle Tea is best served fresh but can be kept in the fridge for up to 24 hours. Reheat slowly without cooking or enjoy cold.

Tips for allergens

Individuals with allergies to pine or similar trees should continue with caution and may want to speak with a healthcare source before trying pine needle tea. Always start with a small amount to test for any bad reactions.

SAGE AND THYME GARGLE

Beneficial effects

Sage and Thyme Gargle is an effective natural treatment for treating sore throats, lowering inflammation, and fighting off bacterial diseases. Sage has antibiotic qualities that can help kill germs that cause throat infections, while thyme contains chemicals like thymol, known for its antibacterial and antifungal effects. This drink can provide quick relief from throat pain and soreness, making it an excellent choice for those suffering from colds, flu, or other breathing conditions.

Ingredients

- One tablespoon of dried sage leaves
- One tablespoon of dried thyme leaves
- 1 cup boiling water
- One teaspoon salt

Instructions

1. Combine the dried sage and thyme leaves in a heat-resistant bowl.

2. Pour 1 cup of hot water over the herbs, ensuring they are fully covered.
3. Cover the bowl and leave the mixture for 20-30 minutes.
4. Strain the juice into another bowl, removing the plant bits.
5. Stir in 1 teaspoon of salt until it melts fully.
6. Allow the solution to cool to a warm, comfortable temperature for gargling.
7. Gargle the warm sage and thyme mix for 30 seconds, then spit it out. For ease, repeat several times a day as needed.

Variations

- Mix a tablespoon of honey in the warm liquids before gargling for extra antibiotic qualities.
- Add a few drops of lemon juice for a vitamin C boost and to add a delicious taste.
- For a stronger rinse, include a clove of crushed garlic in the steeping process. Garlic has powerful antiviral and antibiotic properties.

Storage Tips

Prepare the Sage and Thyme Gargle fresh for each use to ensure strength and effectiveness. It is not recommended to keep the rinse made as the plant's qualities may reduce over time.

Tips for allergens

Individuals with reactions to plants in the Lamiaceae family, which includes both sage and thyme, should continue with caution and may want to speak with a healthcare source before trying this treatment. For those allergic to honey, it can be removed from the change plans.

ECHINACEA: OVERVIEW AND BENEFITS

Echinacea, a name taken from the Greek word 'echinos' meaning sea urchin or hedgehog, mentions the spiky look of its flower heads. This group of leafy plants, part of the daisy family, is native to North America and has been a staple in traditional Native American medicine for ages. The most widely used species for medical reasons include Echinacea purpurea, Echinacea angustifolia, and Echinacea pallida, each known for their unique medicinal qualities. Characterized by their bright pink or purple flowers and middle cones that are generally spiky and dark brown to red, Echinacea plants are visually striking and rich in chemicals helpful to health. The healing benefits of Echinacea are numerous, credited to its complex mix of active substances, including polysaccharides, glycoproteins, alkamides, volatile oils, and flavonoids. These chemicals add to the plant's immune-boosting, anti-inflammatory, and antibacterial traits. Echinacea is most famous for its ability to boost the immune system's reaction, making it a popular treatment for avoiding and healing the common cold, flu, and other lung diseases.

Research shows that Echinacea can reduce the length and sharpness of cold symptoms at the beginning of an illness. Its immune-stimulating effects stem from increasing white blood cell production and activity, which plays a vital part in the body's fight against germs. Beyond its immune-enhancing powers, Echinacea has been studied for its promise in wound healing and skin health due to its anti-inflammatory and antibacterial properties. These qualities make it helpful in the direct treatment of cuts, burns, and other skin conditions, boosting faster mending and lowering the risk of infection. Additionally, Echinacea's antioxidant components add to its health-promoting benefits, helping to remove dangerous free radicals and lower oxidative stress in the body. While Echinacea is usually considered safe for most people, it is essential to consider the amount and time of use to maximize benefits and prevent possible side effects. It is available in various forms, including drinks, pills, drugs, and skin creams, giving freedom in how it can be worked into health and exercise routines. However, people with inflammatory diseases, pregnant or breastfeeding women, and those on certain medicines should speak with a healthcare source before using Echinacea due to possible contraindications and conflicts. Incorporating Echinacea into one's health practice, especially during cold and flu season, can offer a natural and effective way to improve the immune system, fight diseases, and support general well-being. Its long history of use in plant medicine, paired with ongoing study into its health benefits, underscores the lasting value of Echinacea as a critical component of natural health practices.

ELDERBERRY ESSENTIALS

Elderberry, officially known as Sambucus nigra, is a plant that has been respected throughout history for its healing powers. This small, dark purple berry is native to Europe but is also found in North America and Asia. The berries and flowers of the elderberry plant are packed with antioxidants and vitamins that can boost the immune system, making it a choice treatment for colds, flu, and other lung diseases. Elderberries are rich in flavonoids, especially anthocyanins, which are responsible for their deep colour and potent antioxidants that help protect cells from damage. These berries also contain vitamin C, dietary fibre, and phenolic acids. The immune-boosting qualities of elderberry come from its ability to drive the immune system, increasing the production of cytokines that are key to the immune response to fight diseases. This makes elderberry a valuable tool in prevention and the drop in the length and severity of cold and flu symptoms. In addition to its immune-supportive effects, elderberry has been shown to have anti-inflammatory and antibacterial properties. This makes it helpful for colds and the flu and eases symptoms linked with allergies and sinus problems. Its antibacterial traits are particularly effective against different types of influenza, giving a natural means of fighting flu viruses. Elderberry, including syrups, pills, drinks, and powders, can be taken differently. Elderberry juice is one of the most popular goods, often taken at the first sign of cold or flu symptoms. When picking elderberry goods, it's essential to choose those made from the berries and flowers of the Sambucus nigra plant, as other parts of the plant can be deadly if not adequately prepared. While usually considered safe for most people, it's recommended to speak with a healthcare source before starting any new vitamin, especially for pregnant or breastfeeding women, children, and those with inflammatory diseases. Elderberry offers a natural, effective way to support the immune system and improve general health and well-being, reflecting plant medicine's ideals by accepting nature's power for healing.

EUCALYPTUS: USES AND HEALTH BENEFITS

Eucalyptus, a tall tree native to Australia, has spread its roots into global plant medicine thanks to its powerful medical qualities. Recognized by its aromatic leaves, the primary source of its health benefits, eucalyptus is a staple in lung health management, especially for conditions like asthma and allergies. The leaves of the eucalyptus tree contain eucalyptol, also known as 1,8-cineole, a substance widely studied for its ability to reduce inflammation, ease pain, and clear congestion. Eucalyptus offers a natural means to ease lung problems for individuals dealing with asthma. The anti-inflammatory features of eucalyptol can help widen the breathing tubes, improve airflow, and lower the symptoms of asthma.

Additionally, its expectorant powers aid in releasing phlegm and easing coughs, making it helpful for those suffering from acute bronchitis or chronic obstructive lung disease (COPD). Allergies, marked by an excess of the immune system to specific allergens, can lead to symptoms such as coughing, rashes, and nose congestion. Eucalyptus oil, when breathed, works as an anti-inflammatory agent, helping to ease these symptoms. Its antibiotic traits also successfully clean the air, possibly lowering allergens and other germs. Eucalyptus is not limited to internal health problems; it also finds application in external treatments for bruises, cuts, and bug bites, thanks to its antibiotic and cleaning qualities. However, its most significant benefits are noticed in the treatment of breathing conditions, where the eucalyptus plant's leaves and essential oil can be utilized. To harness the benefits of eucalyptus for asthma and allergies, the leaves can be soaked in hot water to make a healing tea, which helps decongest the nose passages and clear the lungs. Eucalyptus essential oil can also be added to hot water for steam absorption. This directly gives helpful chemicals to the respiratory system, easing congestion and improving breathing. It is important to note that while eucalyptus can offer significant relief for asthma and allergic problems, it should not replace approved drugs but serve as a complementary treatment. Individuals with substantial asthma or allergies should speak with a healthcare source before putting eucalyptus into their treatment plan to ensure it is proper for their case. In conclusion, eucalyptus is a natural medicine with various health benefits, especially for those wanting help with breathing conditions such as asthma and allergies. Its anti-inflammatory, expectorant, and antibacterial traits make it a valuable addition to natural health tools, giving a balanced approach to treating these conditions and improving general lung health.

EXPLORING LICORICE: OVERVIEW AND BENEFITS

Licorice, officially known as Glycyrrhiza glabra, is an annual herb native to parts of Europe and Asia. It has been used for thousands of years in different countries for its healing powers, primarily taken from its roots. The name "liquorice" refers to the sweet root of the plant, which includes a chemical called glycyrrhizin, which is up to fifty times sweeter than sugar. This sweetness is not just for taste; glycyrrhizin and other chemicals in liquorice have essential health benefits. Traditionally, liquorice has been employed to treat a wide range of illnesses, from stomach problems to lung issues. Its anti-inflammatory and demulcent features make it particularly effective in soothing sore throats, healing stomach ulcers, and easing abdominal pain. Liquorice root can help reduce acid reflux and heartburn by improving the stomach's mucus lining, providing a safe shield against toxins and acids.

Moreover, liquorice shows expectorant qualities, making it helpful in easing coughs and other respiratory illnesses by speeding the clearance of mucus from the lungs. Its antiviral and antibacterial activities also support the immune system, helping the body to fight off virus diseases and common colds. However, while liquorice offers numerous health benefits, it is crucial to use it carefully. Excessive intake of liquorice or glycyrrhizin can lead to harmful effects, such as hypertension, swelling, and changes in potassium levels. Therefore, it is recommended to consume liquorice in balance and under the direction of a healthcare worker, especially for people with high blood pressure or those taking medicines that may mix with liquorice. Incorporating liquorice into one's diet or plant habit can be done through drinks, pills, or treatments, giving a natural and balanced approach to improving well-being and healing specific health problems. Its long history of use underscores the plant's staying value in herbal medicine, representing the knowledge of old methods updated for modern health challenges.

NETTLE: NAME, DESCRIPTION, AND BENEFITS OF NETTLE.

Nettle, officially known as Urtica dioica, is an annual grass plant utilized for ages across various countries for its wide range of medicinal qualities. This plant, often regarded as a weed in many parts of the world, grows in nitrogen-rich soil and is widely found in Europe, Asia, North America, and parts of Africa. Nettle is marked by its heart-shaped leaves and the fine hairs on its stems and leaves that, upon touch, can give a sting, resulting in short pain and inflammation. This unique defence strategy of the nettle plant is not without purpose; the sting comes from various chemicals, including histamine and formic acid, which have been found to have medical effects. The benefits of Nettle are numerous and cover a broad range of medical uses. Historically, Nettle has been employed internally and externally to treat illnesses ranging from arthritis and anaemia to acne and kidney problems. Internally, nettle tea, made from the plant's dried leaves, is a rich source of vitamins A, C, and K and several B vitamins. It also includes nutrients like calcium, iron, magnesium, phosphorus, potassium, salt, and several antioxidants that protect against cellular damage and oxidative stress. These nutritional components add to the Nettle's standing as a tonic for boosting energy and cleaning the blood. One of the most famous uses of Nettle is in easing urinary tract infections and kidney stones. It works as a diuretic, increasing the flow of pee and helping to flush out dangerous germs and kidney stones from the body.

Additionally, Nettle's anti-inflammatory features make it helpful for lowering the signs of gout and joint pain. The plant's natural antihistamines can also ease seasonal allergies by reducing the amount of histamine the body makes in response to an allergen. Nettle's application goes beyond internal use; externally, Nettle can be applied to the skin to heal cuts, soothe burns, and reduce the strength of skin diseases such as eczema and pimples. Nettle's anti-inflammatory and antibacterial features make it an excellent choice for skin treatments, improving mending and avoiding sickness. Despite its painful nature, Nettle is a plant that offers many benefits for those wanting to work it into their health practice. Whether eaten as a drink, taken in pill form, or applied directly, Nettle's nutritional and medical qualities make it a helpful partner in keeping health and fitness. As with any plant treatment, it is essential to speak with a healthcare source before adding Nettle to your health routine, especially for those with present health problems or those who are pregnant or breastfeeding. Nettle's ability to mix with certain drugs, especially blood thinners and blood pressure meds, shows the need for professional direction in its use. Nonetheless, when used correctly, Nettle stands out as a witness to the power of natural treatments, giving a balanced approach to health that fits with the principles of old plant medicine revived for modern life.

MINT: NAME, DESCRIPTION, AND BENEFITS OF MINT.

Mint, officially known as Mentha, is a widely recognized and beloved vegetable belonging to the Lamiaceae family. This scented plant is native to Europe and Asia but has been spread worldwide due to its varied uses and ease of growth. Mint is marked by its square stem, fast-spreading growth habit, and leaves that release a unique, cooling taste when crushed. Its types, including spearmint (Mentha spicata) and peppermint (Mentha piperita), are the most widely utilized in both food and medical settings. The benefits of Mint spread far beyond its famous use as a mouth cleaner. Mint leaves contain essential oils, including menthol, which are responsible for their cooling feeling. Menthol has painkiller qualities, making Mint a natural cure for easing headaches and muscle pains and lowering the effect of migraines when applied directly as an oil or when breathed. The anti-inflammatory features of Mint also add to its value in soothing stomach troubles. It calms the digestive system's muscles, easing signs of irritable bowel syndrome, including bloating and stomach pain.

Furthermore, Mint is known for its antibiotic and antiviral effects, making it a helpful plant for general immune health. It can help beat common colds by clearing up the blocking of the nose, throat, and lungs. In addition to its healing traits, Mint is rich in nutrients. It is a good source of vitamin A, adding to eye health and night vision. Mint also offers amounts of manganese, essential for bone strength and skin health, and vitamin C, a potent antioxidant that helps the immune system. The herb's refreshing taste and aroma have made it a favourite in food uses worldwide, from teas and drinks to sauces, soups, and sweets. Its cooking freedom and ability to add a new note to recipes are unmatched. Mint's role in mouth health should not be ignored. Its antibiotic features help fight dangerous germs within the mouth, thus avoiding tooth loss and gum diseases. Chewing on mint leaves or rinsing with mint-infused water can improve breath and the mouth area. Cultivating Mint is relatively easy, making it available for home gardening. It grows in wet, well-drained soil and sunny and partly shady places. However, due to its aggressive nature, many farmers prefer to grow Mint in pots to avoid it from overtaking other plants. Harvesting Mint in the morning, when its essential oil content is highest, offers the best taste and strength for food and medicine uses. Incorporating Mint into daily life, whether through food consumption, as a plant cure, or in personal care items, can offer numerous health benefits. Its ease of use and wide range of uses make Mint a helpful herb in the search for natural health and a testament to the lasting knowledge of herbal medicine.

TEN HERBAL REMEDIES FOR TREATING COLDS AND FLU

Elderflower and Peppermint Tea

Beneficial effects

Elderflower and Peppermint Tea is a calm and healing mix ideal for easing symptoms associated with colds and flu. Elderflower acts as a diaphoretic, helping to control heat, while peppermint offers relief from coughs and congestion due to its menthol content. Together, they make a hot tea that helps ease cold symptoms and boosts the immune system.

Ingredients

- Two tablespoons dried elderflowers
- One tablespoon of dried peppermint leaves
- 8 ounces of boiling water
- Honey or lemon (optional, for taste)

Instructions

1. Combine the dried elderflowers and peppermint leaves in a tea bag or straight into a kettle.
2. Pour the hot water over the herbs.
3. Cover and sit for 10-15 minutes to give the taste and health effects to soak.
4. Strain the tea into a cup, removing the elderflowers and peppermint leaves.
5. Add honey or lemon to taste, if desired.
6. Drink warm to feel relief from cold and flu symptoms.

Variations

- For an extra health boost, include a slice of fresh Ginger or a dash of cinnamon in the tea while steeping.
- Mix with a spoonful of elderberry juice to improve antibiotic powers and taste.
- For those wanting a cold beverage, chill the tea and serve with ice cubes for a delicious drink.

Storage Tips

Store any extra dried elderflowers and peppermint leaves in covered containers in a cool, dark place to keep their strength. Prepared Elderflower and Peppermint Tea is best enjoyed fresh but can be kept in the refrigerator for up to 24 hours. Reheat gently before eating.

Tips for allergens

Individuals with allergies to plants in the Asteraceae family, including elderflower and peppermint, should approach with care. Honey can be removed for those with allergies or veggie tastes, and lemon can serve as a plant-based choice for added flavour.

Ginger and Honey Syrup

Beneficial effects

Ginger and Honey Syrup is a potent cure for colds and flu. It uses Ginger's natural anti-inflammatory and antibiotic properties and honey's soothing, antibacterial benefits. This drink can ease sore throats, stop coughing, and boost the immune system, making it an essential addition to your cold and flu season armoury.

Ingredients

- 1 cup of fresh Ginger, peeled and finely grated
- 3 cups of water
- 1 cup of honey

Instructions

1. Combine the chopped Ginger and water in a medium pot. Bring the mixture to a boil over high heat.
2. Reduce the heat to low and cook the ginger-water mixture for about 30 minutes or until the liquid is reduced by half.
3. Strain the liquid through a fine mesh sieve into a heat-resistant bowl, pressing on the ginger grains to remove as much liquid as possible. Discard the ginger solids.
4. While the liquid is still warm (but not boiling), stir in the honey until it is fully dissolved.
5. Allow the syrup to cool to room temperature before moving it to a clean, closed glass bottle or jar.

Variations

- Add a few leaves of thyme or a teaspoon of cinnamon to the cooking stew for extra lung benefits.
- After removing the mixture from the heat, stir in the juice of one lemon to improve its immune-boosting qualities.
- For those choosing a veggie choice, replace honey with maple syrup, raising the sweetness to taste.

Storage Tips

Store the Ginger and Honey Syrup in the refrigerator for up to 3 weeks. Ensure the bottle is covered to maintain its strength and avoid contamination.

Tips for allergens

Individuals with allergies to pollen may respond to honey. In such cases, maple syrup is a safe and effective choice. Always ensure that the Ginger is fresh and mould-free to avoid allergic reactions.

Eucalyptus and Thyme Steam Inhalation

Beneficial effects

Eucalyptus and Thyme Steam Inhalation is a natural and effective way to ease symptoms of colds, flu, and lung illnesses. Eucalyptus includes cineole, a substance known for its antibacterial, anti-inflammatory, and sedative traits. This helps clear nose passages and ease congestion. Thyme, rich in thymol, is a potent antibiotic that can help fight infections and soothe sore throats, making this mix especially helpful for lung health.

Ingredients

- 4 cups of boiling water
- Two tablespoons fresh or dried eucalyptus leaves
- Two tablespoons fresh or dried thyme leaves
- A towel or cloth for covering the head

Instructions

1. Boil 4 cups of water and pour it into a big, heatproof bowl.
2. Add two tablespoons of fresh or dried eucalyptus leaves and two tablespoons of fresh or dried thyme leaves to the hot water.
3. Lean over the bowl, keeping a safe distance to avoid burns, and cover your head and the bowl with a towel to trap the steam.
4. Close your eyes to avoid pain and breathe deeply for 5 to 10 minutes or as long as the steam stays.
5. Repeat 2-3 times daily to relieve congestion, cough, and head pain.

Variations

- Add a few drops of tea tree oil to the water for extra antibiotic benefits.
- If eucalyptus leaves are lacking, 5-10 drops of essential oil can be used as a replacement.

Storage Tips

To preserve their usefulness, fresh eucalyptus and thyme leaves should be kept in the refrigerator, wrapped in a damp paper towel, and put in a plastic bag. Dried eucalyptus and thyme leaves should be kept in sealed containers from direct sunlight and moisture.

Tips for allergens

Individuals with asthma or allergies to eucalyptus, thyme, or other essential oils should continue with caution and may want to speak with a healthcare source before trying this dose. If itching happens, stop using it quickly.

Lemon and Honey Infusion

Beneficial effects

Lemon and Honey Infusion is a healing treatment ideal for treating signs of colds and flu, such as sore throats, coughs, and congestion. The vitamin C in lemon boosts the immune system, while honey has antibiotic effects and can help to coat and soothe a sore throat. This simple yet effective shot can provide quick ease and faster healing.

Ingredients

- One tablespoon of fresh lemon juice
- Two tablespoons of honey
- 1 cup of boiling water

Instructions

1. Boil 1 cup of water and pour it into a mug.
2. Add one tablespoon of fresh lemon juice to the mug.
3. Stir in 2 tablespoons of honey until fully dissolved.
4. Allow the mixture to cool to a safe drinking temperature.
5. Sip the drink slowly to soothe the throat and ease symptoms.

Variations

- Add a slice of fresh Ginger or a dash of cinnamon to the soup for extra anti-inflammatory benefits.
- For extra vitamin C, include a few slices of fresh orange or a dash of orange juice.
- If you prefer a less sweet option, change the amount of honey according to your taste.

Storage Tips

It's best to make the Lemon and Honey Infusion fresh for each use to ensure maximum benefits. However, if you need to make it in advance, store it in a tight jar in the refrigerator for up to 24 hours. Warm gently before drinking.

Tips for allergens

Individuals with pollen allergies should choose prepared honey, as raw honey may contain pollen particles. For those with a citrus phobia, remove the lemon and try using only honey with warm water.

Cinnamon and Clove Tea

Beneficial effects

Cinnamon and Clove Tea is a warming, healing cure for cold and flu season. Its antiviral and antibacterial properties help fight viral and bacterial diseases, while its anti-inflammatory benefits can soothe a sore throat and clear congestion. Cinnamon is known for its ability to boost the immune system, and clove has been used for centuries to reduce pain and inflammation, making this tea a powerful friend against common cold symptoms.

Ingredients

- One cinnamon stick
- Five whole cloves
- 8 ounces of water
- Honey or lemon (optional, for taste)

Instructions

1. Bring 8 ounces of water to a boil in a small pot.
2. Add the cinnamon stick and whole cloves to the hot water.
3. Reduce the heat and cook for 10-15 minutes to allow the spices to taste the water.
4. Remove from heat and strain the tea into a cup, removing the cinnamon stick and cloves.
5. If desired, add honey or a slice of lemon to improve the taste and provide extra vitamin C.
6. Drink warm to enhance relief from cold and flu symptoms.

Variations

- Add a slice of fresh Ginger or a pinch of cayenne pepper while cooking for an extra health boost.
- Mix with an herbal tea bag, such as echinacea or elderberry, during the last few minutes of boiling for extra health benefits.
- Add a star anise pod during cooking and sweeten with maple syrup instead of honey for a sweeter, hotter version.

Storage Tips

The cinnamon sticks and whole cloves can be saved in a covered jar in a cool, dark place for future use. Prepared Cinnamon and Clove Tea is best served fresh but can be kept for up to 24 hours. Reheat gently before eating.

Tips for allergens

Individuals with allergies to cinnamon or cloves should avoid this tea. Honey can be changed with maple syrup for those with allergies or veggie tastes.

Sage and Echinacea Gargle

Beneficial effects

Sage and Echinacea Gargle is a robust plant medicine meant to soothe sore throats, reduce inflammation, and boost the immune system during colds and flu. Sage, known for its antibiotic and anti-inflammatory benefits, works in combination with echinacea, which improves immune function and fights off illnesses. This mix makes a strong rinse that quickly soothes throat pain and supports the body's natural healing processes.

Ingredients

- One tablespoon of dried sage leaves
- One tablespoon of dried echinacea leaves
- 1 cup boiling water
- One teaspoon salt

Instructions

1. Combine the dried sage and echinacea leaves in a heat-resistant bowl.
2. Pour 1 cup of hot water over the herbs, ensuring they are fully covered.
3. Cover the bowl and leave the mixture for 20-30 minutes.
4. Strain the juice into another bowl, removing the plant bits.
5. Stir in 1 teaspoon of salt until it melts fully.
6. Allow the solution to cool to a warm, comfortable temperature for gargling.
7. Gargle the warm sage and echinacea mix for 30 seconds, then spit it out. Repeat several times a day as needed for ease.

Variations

- Mix a tablespoon of honey in the warm liquids before gargling for extra antibiotic qualities.
- Add a few drops of lemon juice for a vitamin C boost and to add a delicious taste.
- For a more vigorous rinse, include a clove of crushed Garlic in the steeping process. Garlic has powerful antiviral and antibiotic properties.

Storage Tips

Prepare the Sage and Echinacea Gargle fresh for each use to ensure strength and effectiveness. It is not recommended to keep the rinse made as the plant's qualities may reduce over time.

Tips for allergens

Individuals with reactions to plants in the Lamiaceae family, which includes sage, or to the Asteraceae family, which provides for echinacea, should continue with caution and may want to speak with a healthcare provider before trying this treatment. For those allergic to honey, it can be removed from the change plans.

Pine Needle and Elderberry Tea

Beneficial effects

Pine Needle and Elderberry Tea is a powerful plant medicine that blends the immune-boosting traits of elderberries with the vitamin C-rich and lung support of pine needles. This tea is beneficial during cold and flu season, as it can help ease symptoms such as coughs, sore throats, and congestion. Elderberry has been shown to shorten the length of colds and flu, while pine needles provide anti-inflammatory benefits and support lung health.

Ingredients

- One tablespoon of dried elderberries
- One tablespoon fresh pine needles, finely chopped (ensure they are from a non-toxic species)
- 8 ounces of boiling water
- Honey or lemon (optional, for taste)

Instructions

1. Place the dried elderberries and finely chopped pine needles in a tea bag or straight into a cup.
2. Pour the hot water over the elderberries and pine leaves.
3. Cover the cup and leave it to sit for 10-15 minutes. This allows the taste and healing benefits to seep into the water.
4. Remove the tea bag or strain the tea to remove the elderberries and pine needles.
5. If desired, add honey or a slice of lemon to improve the taste and provide extra vitamin C.
6. Drink the tea warm, ideally 2-3 times daily, to improve its healing benefits during cold and flu season.

Variations

- For an extra health boost, include a slice of fresh Ginger or a cinnamon stick in the cup while steeping.
- Combine with a small amount of liquorice root to treat the throat.
- Allow the tea to cool and chill for those wanting a cold brew. Serve over ice for a nice, immune-boosting drink.

Storage Tips

Store any extra dried elderberries and pine needles in sealed containers in a cool, dark place to keep their usefulness. Prepared Pine Needle and Elderberry Tea is best enjoyed fresh but can be kept in the refrigerator for up to 24 hours. Reheat gently before eating, or enjoy it cold.

Tips for allergens

Individuals with allergies to pine or blackberry should continue with caution and may want to speak with a healthcare source before trying this tea. Honey can be removed for those with allergies or veggie tastes; maple syrup can be a plant-based sugar replacement.

Garlic and Onion Soup

Beneficial effects

Garlic and Onion Soup uses the strong immune-boosting properties of Garlic and onions. These vegetables are rich in vitamins and have been shown to hold antifungal and antiviral qualities. This soup is warming during cold and flu season and helps lower inflammation, improve cardiac health, and boost the body's immune system.

Ingredients

- Four large onions, thinly sliced
- Four cloves of Garlic, minced
- Two tablespoons of olive oil
- 8 cups of vegetable broth
- One teaspoon of thyme dried
- Salt and pepper to taste
- Four slices of crusty bread
- 1 cup of grated Parmesan cheese

Instructions

1. Heat the olive oil in a big pot over medium heat.
2. Add the sliced onions and cook, stirring occasionally, until they are soft and yellow, about 10 minutes.
3. Add the chopped Garlic and thyme, cooking for another 2 minutes until the Garlic is fragrant.
4. Pour in the veggie stock and bring the mixture to a boil.
5. Reduce the heat and boil for about 20 minutes to allow the taste to mix.
6. Season the soup with salt and pepper to taste.
7. Preheat the grill. Place the pieces of toasted bread on a baking sheet and sprinkle thickly with grated Parmesan cheese.
8. Broil the bread slices until the cheese is melted and bubbly, about 2-3 minutes.
9. To serve, spoon the soup into cups and top each with a cheesy bread slice.

Variations

- Add a cup of chopped carrots or celery with the onions for a heartier version.
- Substitute thyme with rosemary or sage for a different taste mix.
- Veggie option: Omit the Parmesan cheese or replace a veggie cheese to top the bread.

Storage Tips

Garlic and Onion Soup can be saved in a sealed jar in the refrigerator for up to 3 days. Reheat on the stove over medium heat until warm. The cheesy bread should be made fresh for serving.

Tips for allergens

For those with gluten issues, use gluten-free bread for the cheesy bread topping and ensure the veggie soup is gluten-free as well.

Licorice Root and Marshmallow Root Tea

Beneficial effects

Licorice Root and Marshmallow Root tea are peaceful plant medicines known for their ability to ease breathing problems and soothe sore throats, making them excellent choices for cold and flu season. Liquorice root has anti-inflammatory and antibiotic traits that help lower throat swelling and fight germs. In contrast, marshmallow root includes mucilage that coats and protects the nose membranes, easing breathing and itching.

Ingredients

- One teaspoon of dried licorice root
- One teaspoon of dried marshmallow root
- 8 ounces of water
- Honey or lemon (optional, for taste)

Instructions

1. Bring 8 ounces of water to a boil in a small pot.
2. Add one teaspoon of dried liquorice root and one teaspoon of dried marshmallow root to the hot water.
3. Reduce the heat and simmer for 10-15 minutes, allowing the herbs to taste the water.
4. Strain the tea into a cup, removing the herb bits.
5. If desired, add honey or a slice of lemon to improve the taste and provide extra healing benefits.
6. Drink the tea warm, up to three times a day, to ease signs of colds and flu.

Variations

- For extra lung support, include a pinch of dried Ginger or cinnamon in the cooking process.
- Combine with a teaspoon of thyme leaves during boiling for extra medicinal benefits.

Storage Tips

Dried liquorice and marshmallow root should be stored in sealed cases in a cool, dark place to maintain strength. Prepared tea is best served fresh but can be chilled for up to 24 hours. Reheat gently before eating.

Tips for allergens

Individuals with hypertension should be careful when eating liquorice root, as it can affect blood pressure levels. For those with sensitivities or allergies to liquorice or marshmallow plants, consider speaking with a healthcare source before trying this treatment. Honey can be removed for a veggie choice or swapped with maple syrup for sweetness.

Peppermint and Ginger Chest Rub

Beneficial effects

Peppermint and Ginger Chest Rub uses peppermint and Ginger's natural anti-inflammatory and healing traits to ease cold and flu symptoms. Peppermint contains menthol, which can help ease breathing and clear congestion, while Ginger offers cooling and anti-nausea benefits. This mix relieves coughs, lowers lung tightness, and promotes rest during healing.

Ingredients

- ¼ cup coconut oil
- Two tablespoons grated beeswax
- Ten drops of peppermint essential oil
- Ten drops of ginger essential oil
- Five drops of eucalyptus essential oil (optional for added decongestant effect)

Instructions

1. Slowly heat the coconut oil and chopped beeswax together in a double pot until entirely liquid.
2. Remove from heat and allow the liquid to cool slightly but not harden.
3. Carefully stir in the peppermint, Ginger, and eucalyptus essential oils until well mixed.
4. Pour the liquid into a small, sealed jar to cool and harden.
5. Rub a small amount of the chest rub on your chest, neck, and back to ease stiffness and soothe coughs.

Variations

- Lower the amount of essential oil or increase the amount of coconut oil and beeswax to lessen the strength of sensitive skin.
- Add lavender essential oil for its cooling and anti-inflammatory benefits, further helping rest and sleep.

Storage Tips

Store the Peppermint and Ginger Chest Rub in a cool, dry place. If kept properly in a sealed container, it can last for up to 6 months. To maintain the strength of the essential oils, avoid exposure to strong sunlight or high temperatures.

Tips for allergens

Individuals responding to peppermint, Ginger, or eucalyptus should perform a spot test on a small skin area before completing treatment. If itching happens, stop using it quickly. Those allergic to coconut oil can use a different carrier oil, such as almond or olive oil.

HERBS FOR SKIN HEALTH

Herbs have been respected for ages, not only for their medical effects but also for their profound benefits in skin health. The skin, the body's most significant part, serves as the first line of safety against foreign stresses. It's no wonder that old herbalism has a considerable amount of information regarding care for and protecting the face using natural treatments. Among the various herbs helpful for skin health, Calendula, Aloe Vera, Lavender, Burdock, Tea Tree Oil, and Coconut Oil stand out for their unique qualities and usefulness in treating a wide range of dermatological problems. Calendula, known for its bright yellow and orange flowers, holds strong anti-inflammatory and antibacterial qualities, making it an excellent choice for healing cuts, easing eczema, and reducing acne-related inflammation. Its ability to boost collagen production helps the skin's natural repair process, lowering scars and improving skin health and strength. Aloe Vera, a green plant rich in vitamins, minerals, and amino acids, is praised for its cooling, soothing, and healing qualities. It's particularly helpful in healing sunburns, hydrating dry skin, and easing acne and rashes. The gel collected from its leaves is a base for many beauty products, boosting skin growth and providing a safe shield against foreign toxins. With its enchanting taste, lavender is a treat for the senses and a boon for the skin. Its cleaning and anti-inflammatory qualities make it ideal for fighting acne, soothing sensitive skin, and encouraging rest through its calming smell. Lavender oil can be softened and applied directly to heal minor burns, cuts, and bug bites or added to bathwater for a relaxing and healing experience.

Burdock root, recognized in traditional medicine for its blood-purifying effects, has significant benefits for skin health. Its antioxidant and anti-inflammatory traits help heal acne, eczema, and psoriasis, lowering inflammation and improving the general look of the face. Burdock can be eaten as a drink or used as an oil product for direct treatment. Tea Tree Oil, taken from the leaves of the Melaleuca alternifolia tree, is famous for its vigorous cleaning, antifungal, and antibacterial qualities. It's highly beneficial in treating pimples, lowering dandruff, and fixing bacterial illnesses. When using tea tree oil, it's important to mix it with a carrier oil to prevent skin reaction. Coconut Oil, taken from the heart of ripe coconuts, is rich in fatty acids, making it an excellent cleaner for dry skin. Its antibacterial features also help heal various skin diseases, including acne, eczema, and skin infections.

Coconut oil can be used as a natural makeup remover, body lotion, or base for homemade health items. These herbs can be added to your beauty routine through different preparations, such as brews, decoctions, ointments, and essential oils. For instance, making a calendula-infused oil includes steeping dried calendula flowers in a carrier oil, such as almond or olive oil, for several weeks before straining. This oil can then be applied straight to the skin or used as a base for making creams and salves.

Similarly, aloe vera juice can be taken from the plant's leaves straight or mixed with other herbal products to improve its skin-soothing benefits. When utilizing herbs for skin health, it's crucial to consider individual skin types and allergens. Patch testing a small area of the skin before applying plant products is usually suggested to ensure compatibility and prevent unpleasant reactions.

Additionally, finding high-quality, organic herbs and carrier oils is vital to boost the medical benefits and reduce the risk of contaminants. Embracing the knowledge of old herbalism for skin health links us to the natural world and offers a complete and sustainable approach to skincare. By accepting the power of herbs, we can feed, protect, and renew our skin, tapping into the old beauty secrets of our ancestors.

CALENDULA: OVERVIEW AND BENEFITS

Calendula, officially known as Calendula officinalis, is a gem in the world of medicinal herbs, beloved for its bright yellow and orange flowers that reflect a powerhouse of healing qualities. Originating from the Mediterranean, this plant has travelled through the ages, immersing itself in the structure of traditional medicine across different countries. Calendula's flowers, rich in flavonoids and carotenoids, add to its potent anti-inflammatory and antioxidant powers, making it a critical friend in the natural healing kit. The herb's flexibility spreads to various therapeutic uses, especially in skin care and wound healing. Calendula's anti-inflammatory action soothes skin irritations, from diaper rash to eczema, giving gentle yet effective comfort. Its antimicrobial qualities aid in avoiding infection, while its ability to boost collagen production speeds the healing of cuts, burns, and bruises, reducing damage. Beyond outward uses, calendula has been found to support digestive health, easing inflammation in the gut and healing stomach sores. Incorporating calendula into daily health routines can be as simple as putting calendula-infused oil or cream on affected skin areas or making a relaxing tea from its dried leaves. Making calendula tea includes steeping the dried flowers in hot water, which uses its healing benefits and offers peace. As with any herbal treatment, it's essential to approach calendula with care, especially for those with allergies to plants in the Asteraceae family. However, when used with care, marigold stands out as a testament to the staying knowledge of plant medicine, giving a natural, balanced approach to health that fits with the principles of old methods updated for modern well-being. Its gentle efficiency and broad range of uses make calendula a staple in the plant medicine box, reflecting the mending power of nature in every flower.

EXPLORING ALOE VERA: IDENTITY AND BENEFITS

Aloe Vera, known adequately as Aloe barbadensis miller, is a tropical plant species from the genus Aloe. Its leaves are thick and fleshy, green to grey-green, with some types having white flecks on their upper and lower stem surfaces. The tip of the leaf is sharp and has small white teeth. This plant has been used for healing in different countries for millennia, especially in old Egypt, Greece, India, China, Mexico, and Japan. Aloe Vera grows mainly in the dry parts of Africa, Asia, Europe, and America. Due to its wide range of health benefits and ease of growth, Aloe Vera has become one of the most widely used plant treatments worldwide. The benefits of Aloe Vera are numerous and different, covering skin care, gut health, and immune system support.

The gel stored within the leaves is rich in helpful substances, including vitamins, minerals, amino acids, and enzymes. It is this cream that is most generally used for its health benefits. Aloe Vera juice is famous for its cooling, soothing, and healing qualities, making it a staple in skin care for treating burns, sunburns, cuts, and other skin irritations. Its antibiotic properties also help to avoid infection reduction. Beyond its outward uses, Aloe Vera is known for its benefits when eaten. The plant's juice includes several enzymes that help break down sugars and fats, aiding digestion and improving gut health. Its anti-inflammatory and cleaning components are helpful for those with irritable bowel syndrome (IBS) and other inflammatory diseases of the digestive system.

Additionally, aloe vera juice is thought to improve the immune system thanks to its high level of antioxidants, which fight the harmful effects of free radicals. Aloe vera's application in tooth and mouth health is another area of interest, with studies showing that its antibacterial and antibiotic traits can help reduce dental plaque, treat gum diseases, and soothe oral sores.

Moreover, vitamin C in Aloe Vera juice can promote gum health and ease swollen gums. Incorporating Aloe Vera into one's health practice can be done in various ways, from putting the goo straight from the plant to the skin to eating the juice or using things filled with Aloe Vera extract. When using Aloe Vera directly, it's as simple as breaking a leaf open and putting the fresh goo in the affected area. For internal benefits, taking a small amount of Aloe Vera juice every day can support gut health and defence. However, it's important to note that Aloe Vera should be used with care, as having high amounts can have laxative effects and may mix with certain medicines. Despite its wide range of uses and benefits, people should speak with a healthcare provider before adding Aloe Vera into their health practice, especially if they are pregnant, breastfeeding, or have underlying health problems. With its long history of use and a growing amount of scientific study backing its benefits, Aloe Vera continues to be a valuable and flexible component of natural health and wellness practices.

LAVENDER: USES IN SKINCARE AND HEALTH

Lavender, officially known as Lavandula angustifolia, is a widely beloved plant native to the Mediterranean, Middle East, and India, praised for its captivating smell and extensive medical qualities. With its small blue-violet flowers, this annual plant has been utilized for ages in various countries for its calming and healing abilities, making it a choice in traditional and modern herbal medicine. Lavender's flexibility goes beyond its well-known scented uses to a broad range of medical applications, especially in beauty and skin treatments. The benefits of lavender for skin health are deep and varied. Its anti-inflammatory and antibacterial features make it an excellent acne treatment, helping reduce the swelling and redness associated with breakouts and avoiding bacterial infections. When softened and applied directly, lavender oil can ease and heal bug bites, minor burns, and cuts, speeding the skin's healing process by boosting tissue regrowth.

Moreover, its antioxidant components aid in fighting the harmful effects of smog and stress on the skin, possibly avoiding signs of ageing and promoting a young, healthy face. For individuals dealing with skin diseases such as eczema, psoriasis, or dermatitis, lavender can offer significant comfort. Its anti-inflammatory action helps to ease itching and reduce the strength of flare-ups, while its soothing effects prevent the skin from becoming too dry or flaky.

Additionally, lavender's relaxing smell lowers stress, especially since worry can often cause or worsen skin problems. Incorporating lavender into beauty practices is both simple and flexible. Lavender-infused oils can be directly applied to the skin or added to baths for a relaxing and healing experience. A few drops of lavender essential oil can be mixed with a carrier oil and dabbed onto spots for a natural acne cure. Homemade lavender water, formed by steeping the flowers in hot water and then straining, can serve as a gentle face wash or spritz, giving hydration and a refreshing boost throughout the day. Despite its wide range of benefits, using lavender with care is essential, especially for sensitive skin or allergies. Conducting a patch test before broad application can help ensure compatibility and prevent unpleasant effects.

Furthermore, when picking lavender items or essential oils, going for high-quality, pure, and organic choices is crucial to avoid skin irritation caused by artificial additives or chemicals. Lavender's role in skincare displays the perfect mix of beauty, health, and natural healing, reflecting the core of plant medicine's power to support the body and mind. Its continuing use across generations and countries underscores lavender's timeless appeal and effectiveness, making it a valued component of natural health practices and a testament to the ongoing wisdom of nature's medicine.

BURDOCK ESSENTIALS: IDENTITY & BENEFITS

Burdock, officially known as Arctium lappa, is a hardy annual plant well-regarded in different traditional medicine systems for its various health benefits. Originating from Europe and Asia, this plant has since been spread worldwide, praised for its healing benefits and as a food item in Japanese and Korean cuisines. Characterized by its broad leaves and thistle-like purple flowers, burdock is most notable for its long, thin roots that dig deep into the earth. The roots of burdock are where its healing solid powers lie. Rich in inulin, a type of soluble fibre, burdock roots support good digestion and gut bacteria balance. This prebiotic component helps in the growth of helpful bacteria in the gut, adding to better stomach health and immune function.

Additionally, burdock roots contain potent antioxidants, including quercetin, luteolin, and phenolic acids, which help fight oxidative stress and may reduce inflammation. Burdock's watery traits further add to its health benefits, promoting the removal of toxins through greater pee output. This natural cleaning process supports kidney function and may avoid water buildup, making valuable burdock for urinary tract health. Moreover, its blood-purifying powers are widely believed to clear the bloodstream of toxins, possibly helping skin health by lowering acne, eczema, and psoriasis signs. The anti-inflammatory features of burdock make it a natural treatment for joint pain and gout. By reducing inflammation, burdock can ease pain and improve movement for those suffering from these conditions.

Additionally, some studies show that burdock may have anti-cancer traits, with research showing its ability to prevent cancer cell growth, especially in pancreatic and liver cancers. However, more scientific study is needed to fully understand these effects. Incorporating burdock into one's food or health plan can be achieved in different ways. The roots can be eaten fresh or cooked, and they are often found in health food shops or Asian stores. Burdock root tea is another popular way to enjoy its benefits. It is made by steeping dried roots in hot water.

Additionally, burdock is available in supplement form, including pills, drinks, and preparations, making it a handy choice for those looking to harness its medicinal qualities. When using burdock, it's essential to start with small amounts to measure resistance and avoid possible side effects, such as allergic reactions or stomach pain in some people. As with any plant product, speaking with a healthcare provider before adding burdock to your health routine is advised, especially for those with pre-existing conditions or those taking medicines, to avoid dangerous responses. Burdock's various benefits, from promoting gut health to supporting cleaning and lowering inflammation, underscore its value in plant medicine. As a natural drug passed down through generations, burdock reflects the ideas of old herbalism, giving a complete approach to health that fits with the body's natural processes. Its addition to the modern plant medicine cabinet continues to link to the knowledge of traditional healing practices, proving the continued usefulness of nature's pharmacy in supporting health and well-being.

TEA TREE OIL ESSENTIALS

Tea Tree Oil, taken from the leaves of the Melaleuca alternifolia, a native tree of Australia, has been a cornerstone in traditional medicine for ages, valued for its vigorous cleaning and antibacterial and anti-inflammatory properties. This essential oil is distinguished by its camphoraceous taste and ability to treat various conditions, making it a flexible addition to any natural health and fitness practice. Its success is linked to the chemical terpinene-4-ol responsible for most of the tea tree oil's antibiotic and anti-inflammatory effects. The benefits of tea tree oil are vast and well-documented, ranging from beauty uses to treating viruses, bacterial, and fungus diseases. In medicine, tea tree oil is commonly used to fight acne because it reduces redness and removes skin germs. Its application on acne-prone skin can lead to fewer spots and better skin clarity without the roughness of chemical treatments.

Additionally, tea tree oil helps heal fungal diseases such as athlete's foot, nail fungus, and yeast infections, giving a natural choice to over-the-counter antifungal drugs. Beyond its health benefits, tea tree oil has been shown to heal lung problems. When used in massage, it can help ease congestion, lessen the signs of colds, and soothe sore throats. Its antiviral qualities also make it a valuable tool in avoiding viral illnesses, with studies showing its success in inactivating virus particles when used as a surface cleaner or in hand sanitizers. Tea tree oil offers a natural answer for skin problems such as acne or lice. Its ability to ease an itchy scalp, reduce dandruff, and clear lice has made it a popular ingredient in natural hair care products. Tea tree oil can improve skin health when wet and applied to the head, leading to stronger, thicker hair. Despite its various benefits, using tea tree oil properly is vital. It should always be mixed with a carrier oil, such as coconut or olive oil, to avoid skin redness. Direct application of pure tea tree oil can lead to unpleasant reactions, including swelling, itchiness, and burning, especially in people with sensitive skin.

Tea tree oil should never be eaten due to its possible danger. Incorporating tea tree oil into daily jobs is easy. A few drops can be added to a carrier oil or cream for skin use and applied straight to the affected area. For lung relief, adding a few drops to a bowl of hot water and breathing the air can provide phlegm relief. As a natural cleaning agent, it can be mixed with water and vinegar to make a strong, non-toxic cleaner for surfaces. Tea tree oil shows the power of natural drugs, connecting old medical practices and modern-day health and exercise needs. Its broad range of uses and benefits underscores the freedom and usefulness of plant medicine, making it an essential component of any natural health tool.

EXPLORING COCONUT OIL: USES AND BENEFITS

Coconut oil, taken from the ripe fruit of the coconut tree (Cocos nucifera), is a fantastic product in the world of natural health and fitness. Its unique makeup, rich in medium-chain triglycerides (MCTs), especially lauric acid, makes it a potent antibiotic agent capable of warding off bacteria, viruses, and fungi. This oil has been respected in various cultures, especially in warm areas with abundant coconut trees, for its nutritional value and extensive medical qualities. The benefits of coconut oil are varied, covering internal and outward uses. Internally, coconut oil can improve metabolism and provide a quick energy source due to its MCT level. It helps the immune system thanks to its lauric acid, which the body changes into monolaurin, a chemical known for its ability to fight germs.

Additionally, it has been shown to improve cholesterol levels by increasing the amount of high-density lipoprotein (HDL) cholesterol, thereby boosting heart health. Externally, coconut oil is equally helpful. Its healing features make it an excellent natural dry skin and hair treatment. Thanks to its anti-inflammatory and healing benefits, it can directly help eczema, psoriasis, and other skin problems. Furthermore, coconut oil is used in oil pulling, a traditional Ayurvedic method that includes swishing the oil in the mouth to remove bacteria, improve oral health, and even whiten teeth. In the kitchen, coconut oil is a flexible food oil with a high smoke point, making it great for frying, baking, and sautéing. Its unique taste adds a tropical twist to meals, while its nutritional profile helps a healthy diet. Despite its wide range of uses and benefits, it's important to use coconut oil in balance, especially when eaten, as it is high in fatty fats. Opting for pure coconut oil, which is less handled, can ensure that you're getting the most natural and healthy product. Incorporating coconut oil into daily habits, whether for food reasons, skin and hair care, or as part of a balanced approach to health, can offer significant benefits. Its natural qualities meet the ideals of plant medicine, stressing avoidance, natural healing, and the use of whole, raw substances to support the body's health and well-being.

TEN HERBAL REMEDIES FOR SKIN HEALTH

Calendula Salve

Beneficial effects

Calendula Salve is famous for its unique healing qualities, especially in treating skin irritations, cuts, and dry skin conditions. Its anti-inflammatory, antibacterial, and antifungal features make it an excellent choice for improving skin health and speeding mending. This balm can soothe eczema, psoriasis, diaper rash, and chapped skin, making it a flexible addition to any natural skincare routine.

Ingredients

- 1 cup of calendula-infused oil (made by steeping dried calendula petals in a carrier oil like olive or almond oil for several weeks)
- 1/4 cup of beeswax pellets
- Two tablespoons of shea butter
- Ten drops of lavender essential oil (optional for added antimicrobial and soothing properties)
- Five drops of tea tree essential oil (optional for enhanced antiseptic benefits)

Instructions

1. Begin by making a double pot. Fill a pot with a few inches of water and place it on the stove over medium heat.
2. Mix the calendula-infused oil, beeswax pellets, and shea butter in a heat-resistant bowl that fits snuggly over the pot.

3. Allow the mixture to melt together, shaking occasionally to ensure even mixing.
4. Carefully remove the bowl from the heat once the mixture is fully melted and mixed.
5. Stir in the lavender and tea tree essential oils, if using, until thoroughly mixed.
6. Pour the mixture into small tins or jars. Let it cool and solidify at room temperature.
7. Once solid, cover the cases with lids to keep the balm.

Variations

- Add a tablespoon of coconut oil to the mix during the melting process for extra healing benefits.
- Incorporate vitamin E oil as a natural antioxidant and skin-nourishing agent. After pulling the liquid from the heat, add a teaspoon.
- Customize the balm with different essential oils based on your skin's needs or tastes. Chamomile is used for extra mending, rosehip is used for renewal, and frankincense is used for aged skin.

Storage Tips

Store the Calendula Salve in a cool, dry place away from direct sunlight. If kept properly, the medicine can last for up to a year. However, natural things may lose some of their power over time, so it's best used within the first few months for the most significant benefits.

Tips for allergens

For those with allergies to beeswax, a plant-based wax like candelilla can be used. Always perform a spot test before putting new things on the skin, primarily if you have known allergies or sensitivities. Essential oils can be removed or changed based on personal tolerance and taste.

Aloe Vera Gel

Beneficial effects

Aloe Vera Gel is famous for its cooling, soothing, and healing qualities, making it an excellent option for skin health. It can help treat sunburn, hydrate the skin, speed wound healing, and even reduce acne and redness. Its rich mix of vitamins, minerals, and antioxidants can support the skin's general health and protect against exterior pressures.

Ingredients

- One large Aloe Vera leaf
- One teaspoon of Vitamin E oil (optional for added skin nourishment)

Instructions

1. Carefully slice off the sharp edges of the Aloe Vera leaf.
2. Slowly remove the transparent, gel-like material inside the leaf with a knife or spoon and put it in a clean bowl.
3. Add the Vitamin E oil to the bowl with the Aloe Vera juice.
4. Mix the gel and Vitamin E oil using a mixer or a fork until you achieve a smooth consistency.
5. Transfer the Aloe Vera juice into a sealed jar for storage.

Variations

- Mix a few drops of tea tree oil into the Aloe Vera gel for an anti-acne gel for its antifungal properties.

- Add a few drops of lavender essential oil, which is ideal for use before sleep, to enhance the relaxing effects.
- Mix the Aloe Vera gel with a few tablespoons of coconut oil for extra moisture.

Storage Tips

Store the aloe vera juice in a covered jar in the refrigerator for up to one week. For longer storage, freeze the gel in ice cube trays and thaw as needed.

Tips for allergens

Individuals allergic to aloe vera should perform a spot test on a small skin area before applying it extensively. Vitamin E oil can be deleted for those who are allergic to it.

Chamomile and Lavender Skin Soother

Beneficial effects

Chamomile and Lavender Skin Soother is a gentle, natural treatment for irritated skin, reducing inflammation and promoting healing. Chamomile, known for its anti-inflammatory and antioxidant properties, works to relax the skin, while lavender, celebrated for its cleaning and anti-inflammatory qualities, aids in healing and provides a calming smell. This mixture is beneficial for treating conditions like eczema, psoriasis, and other skin irritations and for cooling and improving skin health.

Ingredients

- Two tablespoons of dried chamomile flowers
- Two tablespoons of dried lavender buds
- 1 cup boiling water
- One tablespoon honey (optional for added moisturizing benefits)
- One tablespoon of aloe vera gel (optional for soothing and healing properties)

Instructions

1. Place the dried chamomile flowers and lavender buds in a heat-resistant bowl.
2. Pour 1 cup of hot water over the herbs, ensuring they are fully covered.
3. Cover the bowl and leave the mixture for 15-20 minutes.
4. Strain the mixture, remove the herbs, and move the juice into a clean container.
5. If using, stir in the honey and aloe vera gel until thoroughly melted and mixed.
6. Allow the mixture to cool to room temperature.
7. Apply the skin soother to the trouble area with a clean cotton pad or spray bottle. Gently pat the face dry after treatment.

Variations

- Put the skin soother in the refrigerator before use for extra cooling effects.
- Add a few drops of tea tree oil for its antifungal traits, which are helpful for acne-prone skin.
- For a thicker consistency, blend the cooled mixture with a small amount of coconut oil, which can further aid in healing dry skin.

Storage Tips

Store the Chamomile and Lavender Skin Soother in a covered jar in the refrigerator for up to one week. Ensure the bottle is clean and pure to prevent contamination.

Tips for allergens

Individuals responding to chamomile, lavender, or aloe vera should perform a spot test on a small skin area before completing treatment or speaking with a healthcare source. Honey can be removed for those with allergies or veggie tastes, and aloe vera gel can be changed with an equal amount of cucumber juice for its healing effects.

Neem and Turmeric Face Mask

Beneficial effects

The Neem and Turmeric Face Mask mix Neem's substantial antibacterial and anti-inflammatory benefits with turmeric's antioxidant and skin-brightening effects. This natural method successfully treats acne, lowers scars, and improves general skin health. Neem, known for fighting skin infections and diseases, works closely with turmeric to soothe itching, reduce apparent signs of age, and restore the skin's natural glow.

Ingredients

- Two tablespoons of neem powder
- One tablespoon of turmeric powder
- 3-4 tablespoons of water or aloe vera gel for sensitive skin

Instructions

1. Mix the neem and turmeric powder in a clean bowl until well-mixed.
2. Gradually add water or aloe vera gel to the powder mixture, stirring constantly to form a smooth paste. Adjust the amount of liquid to achieve the desired density.
3. Apply the mask evenly over a clean face, avoiding the area around the eyes and mouth.
4. Leave the mask on for 10-15 minutes or until it dries.
5. Rinse off the mask with cold water, gently rubbing it circularly to cleanse the face.
6. Pat the skin dry with a soft towel and follow up with a lotion fit for your skin type.

Variations

- For dry skin, add a teaspoon of honey to the mix for its soothing benefits.
- Include a few drops of tea tree oil for better antibiotic action, especially for acne-prone skin.
- Add some finely ground oatmeal to the mask mixture for extra cleaning.

Storage Tips

To protect their usefulness, store extra neem and turmeric powders in covered cases in a cool, dry place. The mask mix should be made fresh each time to ensure speed and prevent spoiling.

Tips for allergens

Individuals with sensitivity to Neem or turmeric should perform a patch test on a small area of skin before applying the mask to the entire face. If you have sensitive skin, replace the water with aloe vera juice for a kinder choice.

Rosehip Seed Oil Serum

Beneficial effects

Rosehip Seed Oil Serum is famous for its excellent skin-rejuvenating qualities, making it a valuable addition to any skincare program focused on improving skin health. Rich in essential fatty acids, vitamins A and C, and antioxidants, this cream can help soothe the skin, reduce signs of age such as wrinkles and fine lines, and improve skin tone and structure. Additionally, its anti-inflammatory benefits can aid in reducing redness and itching, making it great for those with sensitive skin conditions.

Ingredients

- Two tablespoons rosehip seed oil
- 1 tablespoon jojoba oil
- Five drops of lavender essential oil
- Two drops of frankincense essential oil
- Dark glass dropper bottle

Instructions

1. Mix two tablespoons of rosehip seed oil in a clean bowl with one tablespoon of jojoba oil. These carrier oils serve as the base of your serum, providing deep moisturization and allowing the essential oils to be absorbed.
2. Add five drops of lavender essential oil to the liquid. Lavender oil is known for its cooling and anti-inflammatory benefits, which can help soothe the face and reduce redness.
3. Incorporate two drops of frankincense essential oil. Frankincense is praised for supporting healthy cell regrowth and protecting skin cells, which can help lower the look of scars, fine lines, and wrinkles.
4. Mix the oils properly to ensure they are well mixed.
5. Carefully pour the serum into a dark glass dropper bottle to keep the oils from light, which can damage their quality over time.
6. To apply, place 2-3 drops of the serum onto clean fingers and slowly rub into the face and neck, focusing on areas with fine lines or tightness. Use in the evening before bed to allow the serum to work overnight.

Variations

- Include a few drops of vitamin E oil for extra nutrition, which can also extend the shelf life of your serum.
- If targeting dark spots or uneven skin tone, add a few drops of lemon essential oil for its natural whitening qualities. Lemon oil can increase photosensitivity; use this form in your nighttime practice.

Storage Tips

Store your Rosehip Seed Oil Serum in a cool, dark place to protect the oils' power. When stored properly, the serum can last up to 6 months. Ensure the dropper bottle is tightly shut after each use to prevent rusting.

Tips for allergens

Individuals responding to essential oils should perform a patch test on a small skin area before spreading the liquid widely. Lavender and frankincense oils are usually well-tolerated, but if itching occurs, try lowering or removing the vital oils.

Witch Hazel and Tea Tree Toner

Beneficial effects

Witch Hazel and Tea Tree Toner is an effective natural treatment for improving skin health, especially for those with oily, acne-prone, or sensitive skin. Witch hazel is a natural cleaner, helping close pores and lowering redness. At the same time, tea tree oil offers strong antibiotic and cleaning qualities, making it ideal for avoiding and healing acne breakouts. This toner can soothe sensitive skin, reduce pimples, and promote a healthier face.

Ingredients

- ½ cup witch hazel extract
- ¼ cup distilled water
- Ten drops of tea tree essential oil
- Five drops of lavender essential oil (optional for additional soothing properties)

Instructions

1. Mix the witch hazel oil and pure water in a clean bottle.
2. Add the tea tree essential oil to the mix. If using, add the lavender essential oil for its relaxing and healing benefits on the face.
3. Cap the bottle and shake well to ensure all items are thoroughly mixed.
4. Add the toner to a cotton pad and gently swipe over the cleaned face, avoiding the eye area. For best results, use morning and night.

Variations

For dry skin, try adding a teaspoon of aloe vera gel to the mix for its healing benefits.

If dealing with staining, include a few drops of lemon essential oil for its natural brightening effects. Note that lemon oil can raise photosensitivity, so apply sunscreen before going outdoors.

Storage Tips

Store the Witch Hazel and Tea Tree Toner in a cool, dark place. If kept properly, the toner can last for up to 6 months. Ensure the cap is tightly shut after each use to maintain the strength of the essential oils.

Tips for allergens

Individuals with sensitive skin should perform a patch test before using the wash widely, as tea tree oil can be substantial. If pain happens, reduce the combination with more clean water or stop using. For those allergic to lavender, remove this essential oil from the recipe.

Oatmeal and Honey Exfoliating Scrub

Beneficial effects

The Oatmeal and Honey Exfoliating Scrub is a natural, gentle cleaner that removes dead skin cells, leaving the skin soft and refreshed. Oatmeal has anti-inflammatory and healing effects, making it great for sensitive skin. At the same time, honey is a natural humectant that soothes the face and has antibiotic qualities to help clear impurities.

Ingredients

- 1/2 cup ground oatmeal
- 1/4 cup honey
- 1/4 cup coconut oil, melted
- One tablespoon of lemon juice (optional for additional skin-brightening benefits)

Instructions

1. Mix the ground oatmeal, honey, and melted coconut oil in a medium-sized bowl until well-mixed.
2. Add the lemon juice to the mix for extra face-lightening effects.
3. Apply the scrub to wet skin in a circular motion, focusing on areas with dry skin or rough spots.
4. Rinse off with warm water and pat the face dry with a soft towel.
5. Follow up with your regular cream to lock in moisture.

Variations

- Add a few drops of tea tree oil for acne-prone skin for its antifungal properties.
- Include a teaspoon of ground coffee or spice to make a more stimulating scrub.
- Add a tablespoon of almond or jojoba oil to the blend for extra hydration.

Storage Tips

Any extra scrub can be stored in a sealed jar in the refrigerator for up to one week. Ensure the bottle is closed correctly to prevent the ingredients from spoiling.

Tips for allergens

Individuals with gluten issues should ensure that the oatmeal used is proven gluten-free. For those with allergies to nuts, avoid adding almond oil and consider moving to another skin-friendly oil like sunflower oil.

Comfrey and Plantain Healing Balm

Beneficial effects

Comfrey and Plantain Healing Balm is a powerful, natural medicine for easing and healing skin irritations, cuts, and minor burns. Comfrey, known for its high allantoin content, supports cell growth and skin repair, making it an excellent choice for speeding up the healing process. Rich in anti-inflammatory and antibiotic properties, plantain offers relief from itching and helps avoid illnesses. These herbs form a compelling mix that supports skin health and speeds repair.

Ingredients

- 1/4 cup dried comfrey leaves
- 1/4 cup dried plantain leaves

- 1/2 cup coconut oil
- 1/4 cup beeswax pellets
- Optional: 10 drops of lavender essential oil for added antimicrobial and soothing properties

Instructions

1. Begin by soaking the coconut oil with dried comfrey and plantain leaves. Combine the herbs and coconut oil in a double pot and gently heat on low heat for 2-3 hours, ensuring the oil does not boil.
2. After soaking, squeeze the oil through a napkin to remove the herb bits, squeezing out as much oil as possible. Discard the leaves.
3. Return the combined oil to the double pot and add the beeswax pellets. Heat slowly, stirring occasionally, until the beeswax is fully melted and mixed with the oil.
4. Remove from heat and, if using, stir in the lavender essential oil.
5. Quickly pour the mixture into small tins or jars before it begins to solidify.
6. Allow the balm to cool and set fully, which may take several hours.

Variations

- Add a few drops of tea tree oil for extra healing power for its cleaning properties.
- If beeswax is scarce, you can substitute the same amount of shea butter for a softer balm.

Storage Tips

Store the Comfrey and Plantain Healing Balm in a cool, dry place. If kept properly, it can last for up to a year. Avoid exposing it to strong sunlight or heat to preserve the healing qualities of the oils and herbs.

Tips for allergens

Shea butter is a safe choice for those who react to beeswax. If you are allergic to lavender, remove the essential oil or replace it with another skin-friendly crucial oil like chamomile, which has healing properties.

Green Tea and Cucumber Eye Gel

Beneficial effects

Green Tea and Cucumber Eye Gel mix the antioxidant benefits of green tea with cucumber's cooling and healing effects. This natural treatment is meant to reduce puffiness, soothe tired eyes, and lessen the look of dark circles. Green tea is rich in polyphenols that help protect the delicate skin around the eyes from oxidative stress, while cucumber provides a cooling effect that can help reduce swelling and refresh the face.

Ingredients

- 1/2 cup distilled water
- One tablespoon of green tea leaves
- 1/2 cucumber, peeled and pureed
- One tablespoon of Aloe vera gel
- One teaspoon of vitamin E oil
- 1/2 teaspoon cornstarch

Instructions

1. In a small pot, bring the filtered water to a boil. Remove from heat and add the green tea leaves. Cover and steep for 10 minutes.
2. Strain the tea leaves and allow the green tea to cool to room temperature.
3. Combine the cold green tea, cucumber juice, aloe vera gel, and vitamin E oil in a mixer. Blend until smooth.
4. Transfer the liquid to a small pot and whisk in the cornstarch.
5. Heat the mixture over low heat, turning frequently, until it thickens to a gel-like consistency.
6. Remove from heat and allow the gel to cool thoroughly.
7. Once cooled, move the eye goo to a clean, sealed container.

Variations

- Store the eye gel in the refrigerator before use for extra cooling and healing benefits.
- Add a few drops of lavender essential oil for its relaxing features and pleasant smell.
- Substitute green tea with chamomile tea for its anti-inflammatory benefits, especially for sensitive skin around the eyes.

Storage Tips

Store the Green Tea and Cucumber Eye Gel in a covered jar in the refrigerator for up to 1 week. Ensure the bottle is clean to avoid any germ growth.

Tips for allergens

For those responding to aloe vera or vitamin E oil, perform a skin test on a small face area before putting the gel around the eyes. If pain happens, rinse off quickly and stop use.

Marshmallow Root and Licorice Root Moisturizer

Beneficial effects

Marshmallow Root and Licorice Root Moisturizer is a highly hydrating and healing mix meant to feed and protect the face. Marshmallow root provides a covered layer that helps keep wetness and soothe pain, making it ideal for dry, swollen, or sensitive skin. Liquorice root is known for improving the face, reducing pimples, offering anti-inflammatory benefits, and helping to calm redness and swelling. These herbs make a potent cream that promotes skin health, restoring balance and improving the skin's natural glow.

Ingredients

- ¼ cup dried marshmallow root
- ¼ cup dried licorice root
- 1 cup distilled water
- ½ cup shea butter
- ¼ cup coconut oil
- Two tablespoons of jojoba oil
- One tablespoon beeswax
- Ten drops of lavender essential oil (optional for scent and additional soothing properties)

Instructions

1. Combine the marshmallow root, liquorice root, and distilled water in a small pot. Bring to a boil, then cook for 20-30 minutes to make a strong plant tea.

2. Strain the broth, remove the leaves, and keep the juice.
3. In a double pot, heat the shea butter, coconut oil, jojoba oil, and beeswax together until thoroughly mixed.
4. Remove from heat and slowly mix in the plant liquid, stirring constantly to ensure a smooth combination.
5. Once slightly cooled, add the lavender essential oil, if using, and stir well.
6. Pour the mixture into clean, dry jars or tins and allow to cool fully. The cream will harden as it cools.
7. Label your containers and keep them in a cool, dry place.

Variations

- For extra hydration, add a tablespoon of aloe vera gel to the drink during step 5.
- If you prefer a meatless product, replace the beeswax with equal candelilla wax.
- Add a teaspoon of vitamin E oil to the lavender essential oil for an antioxidant boost.

Storage Tips

The Marshmallow Root and Licorice Root Moisturizer can be stored at room temperature for six months. If your home is hot, keep it in the refrigerator to maintain stability and extend its shelf life.

Tips for allergens

Those who respond to coconut oil can change it with another carrier oil, such as almond or olive oil. Always perform a small test before spreading the cream widely, especially if you have sensitive skin or plant allergies.

HEART-HEALTHY HERBS

The heart, an organ that constantly sends life through our blood, is at the core of our well-being and energy. In natural medicine, numerous plants have been respected for their circulatory benefits, supporting heart health through ages of traditional use and current scientific study. Among these, Hawthorn stands out for its amazing ability to support the heart, a testament to its long history in plant tales and medicine. Hawthorn, officially known as Crataegus species, has been utilized across different countries for its heart-strengthening qualities. Hawthorn's berries, leaves, and flowers are rich in flavonoids and oligomeric proanthocyanidins. These strong vitamins help widen blood vessels, improve blood flow, and protect against blood vessel damage. This joint action adds to blood pressure control, the drop in heart-related chest pains, and the increase in general vascular function. The practice of using Hawthorn for heart health can be traced back to the first century, with its mention in different pharmacopoeias and herbal compendiums throughout history, underscoring its respected place in the herbal medicine cabinet. Garlic, another cornerstone of blood health, has been eaten for its healing benefits since ancient times. Known officially as Allium sativum, Garlic's health benefits are linked to its sulfur-containing chemicals, such as allicin. These substances are thought to have different circulatory benefits, including lowering high blood pressure, cutting cholesterol levels, and avoiding atherosclerosis. The widespread use of Garlic in foods worldwide speaks to its mobility and the ease with which it can be added to a heart-healthy diet. With its formal name, Zingiber officinale, Ginger is another herb praised for its medical qualities, especially its anti-inflammatory and antioxidative benefits. These traits are important for heart health, as inflammation and oxidative stress are key factors in cardiovascular disease. Ginger's ability to improve blood circulation, lower cholesterol, and avoid blood clots makes it a useful partner in having a healthy heart. Its freedom in food use further improves its appeal, allowing for easy integration into daily nutrition. The journey through the garden of heart-healthy herbs is far from over, with each plant having a unique mix of benefits that add to cardiovascular wellness. From the antioxidant-rich Hawthorn to the cholesterol-lowering Garlic and the circulation-boosting Ginger, these herbs show the old knowledge of herbal medicine, giving natural answers for supporting heart health. As we travel deeper into the natural world, we find more about how these plants can be handled to support our hearts, ensuring that the beat goes on, strong and steady. Olive leaves, known officially as Olea europaea, have been regarded for their heart-protective traits, drawing from a rich history of use in Mediterranean countries. The main ingredient, oleuropein, found widely in olive leaves, shows strong antioxidant, anti-inflammatory, and disease-fighting features. These traits add greatly to the circulation system's health by improving heart artery health, reducing the chance of cholesterol, and lowering blood pressure. Incorporating olive leaf extract into the diet can support keeping good blood fat levels, a key factor in avoiding heart disease and strokes. The Horse Chestnut, or Aesculus hippocastanum, is another useful plant in circulatory health. Traditionally used to treat venous insufficiency, horse chestnut strengthens the veins and reduces the permeability of the vessels, thereby helping reduce stiffness and inflammation in the legs. The active component, aescin, has been shown to improve venous tone, boost blood flow back to the heart, and reduce signs of varicose veins and haemorrhoids, often linked with arterial stress. With its bright flowers, Hibiscus is a visual treat and a force of vitamins. Hibiscus sabdariffa is particularly known for its ability to lower high blood pressure, a major risk factor for heart disease. The antioxidants present in Hibiscus, including anthocyanins and flavonoids, have been found to have vasodilatory effects, which help in reducing blood pressure levels. Regular intake of hibiscus tea can be a delightful and effective way to support heart health, offering a simple yet powerful natural answer for maintaining cardiovascular wellness. Integrating these plants into daily life can be a safe and healing way to heart health. For instance, olive leaf extract can be taken in pill form or as a tea, horse chestnut is available in creams for skin application or in tablets for internal use, and Hibiscus can be enjoyed as a pleasant, cold or hot tea. It's important to note that while these herbs offer significant benefits, they should support a heart-healthy lifestyle that includes a balanced diet, regular physical exercise, and stress management practices. Incorporating heart-healthy plants into one's diet suggests a step towards taking the old knowledge of herbalism with a modern understanding of its relevance to current health issues. As we continue to explore the vast plant world, the ability of herbs to support and improve heart health remains an important tool in the quest for healing and energy. By carefully adding these natural methods, people can harness the power of plants to support their hearts, ensuring a strong and healthy circulation system for years to come.

HAWTHORN ESSENTIALS: IDENTITY AND BENEFITS

Hawthorn, officially known as Crataegus species, is a plant rooted in a rich blend of myth and medical history, loved across cultures for its potent effects on heart health. This annual plant, belonging to the rose family, is marked by its thorny branches, deeply lobed leaves, groups of pink or white flowers, and bright red berries or haws. The healing power of Hawthorn lies in its leaves, flowers, and berries, which have been utilized in traditional medicine for ages to treat different blood conditions. The medicinal worth of Hawthorn is mainly linked to its rich mix of flavonoids, oligomeric proanthocyanidins, and other phenolic substances. These helpful ingredients are vital vitamins that produce a vasodilatory effect, improving blood flow and oxygen supply to the heart. By dilating coronary veins, Hawthorn supports lowering blood pressure and alleviates angina, a condition marked by chest pain caused by reduced blood flow to the heart.

Moreover, its antioxidant qualities aid in removing free radicals, thereby protecting against blood vessel damage and adding to general vascular health. Hawthorn's benefits stretch beyond its circulation support and show a slight cooling effect, lowering nervousness and promoting rest. This calming effect and its health benefits make Hawthorn a complete treatment for stress-induced heart problems.

Additionally, Hawthorn has been shown to improve the heart's working efficiency by improving cardiac output, which is especially helpful for those with heart failure, where the heart cannot pump properly to meet the body's needs. The positive use of Hawthorn is flexible, ranging from regular preparations and drugs to drinks and pills, allowing for ease of incorporation into daily health practices. Its safety rate is commendably high, with few known side effects, making it a suitable supplemental medicine for those seeking natural support for heart health. However, despite its benefits, people on heart drugs should speak with a healthcare provider before adding Hawthorn into their routine to avoid possible conflicts. In accepting the old knowledge of herbalism, Hawthorn reflects on plants' ongoing tradition in the natural medicine world. Its multiple benefits show the complete method of plant medicine, which focuses on treating symptoms and supporting general well-being. As we continue to study the mutual relationship between people and plants, Hawthorn remains a light of hope for those looking to improve their heart health naturally, reflecting the spirit of old methods renewed for modern well-being.

GARLIC: NAME, DESCRIPTION, AND BENEFITS OF GARLIC.

Garlic, officially known as Allium sativum, is a plant that belongs to the Allium (onion) family. It is closely related to onions, shallots, and leeks. This spherical plant reaches about 1 meter in height and produces hermaphrodite flowers. Its bulb, the most widely used part of the plant, is split into numerous pieces called cloves. Garlic is native to Central Asia and northeastern Iran and has been used for food and healing for thousands of years. The history of Garlic's use goes back to old societies, including the Egyptians, Babylonians, Greeks, Romans, and Chinese, who valued it for its healing benefits and as a food ingredient. Garlic's healing qualities are mainly linked to sulfur chemicals that form when a garlic clove is chopped, crushed, or eaten. These chemicals include allicin, which is highly helpful but also responsible for Garlic's unique taste. Garlic is famous for its vast collection of health benefits. It has been scientifically proven to boost the immunity system, helping to fight colds and illnesses. Allicin, in particular, has been shown to have strong antibiotic, antiviral, and antifungal traits, making Garlic a natural cure for improving the body's protection against disease.

Additionally, Garlic is known for its circulation benefits. It can help lower blood pressure and cholesterol levels, reducing heart disease risk. The antioxidants in Garlic also protect against cell damage and ageing, possibly cutting the chance of Alzheimer's disease and dementia.

Moreover, Garlic's anti-inflammatory features make it helpful for reducing illnesses linked with inflammation, such as gout. Its ability to improve cleansing processes helps avoid certain cancers by stopping the formation of cancer-causing chemicals, enhancing DNA repair, and inducing cell death in cancer cells. Garlic is also known for improving bone health by increasing estrogen levels in females, which can be particularly helpful in lowering the risk of osteoporosis. Incorporating Garlic into the diet is easy due to its flexibility as a food element. It can be eaten raw or cooked, added to meals for flavour, or taken in supplement form for those who wish to avoid its strong taste. When making Garlic for its health benefits, it's recommended to crush or chop the pieces and let them sit for a few minutes before cooking. This process allows for the formation of allicin, increasing its health benefits. Despite its numerous advantages, garlic-eating may not be ideal for everyone. It can mix with certain drugs, including blood thinners, and may cause side effects such as heartburn, gas, and vomiting in some people. Therefore, it's suggested that you speak with a healthcare source before putting high amounts of Garlic into the diet, especially for those with known health problems or those taking medicine. Garlic stands as a testament to the power of natural drugs, representing the goals of old herbalism in supporting health and well-being. Its broad use throughout history and across countries shows its value as a powerful, natural drug. As we continue to explore and prove the benefits of plant drugs, Garlic remains a cornerstone of natural health, offering a simple yet powerful tool for improving general wellness.

GINGER: BENEFITS AND BLOOD PRESSURE MANAGEMENT

Ginger, officially known as Zingiber officinale, is a growing plant whose base, ginger root, has been widely used for its taste, food, and healing qualities. This flexible plant, native to Southeast Asia, has been a staple in traditional and folk medicine for ages and is praised for its healing effects. Ginger's unique taste and health benefits have made it a beloved spice worldwide, beating culture and food limits. The root of the ginger plant is rich in natural substances, including gingerols, shogaols, and zingerone, which are associated with its potent anti-inflammatory and antioxidant qualities. These helpful chemicals add to ginger's ability to ease nausea, improve gut health, and lower pain. Among its various health benefits, ginger's role in reducing blood pressure is exciting, allowing a natural approach to cardiovascular health. High blood pressure, or hypertension, is a common problem that offers significant health risks, including heart disease and stroke. Managing blood pressure is essential for keeping heart health and avoiding these dangerous effects. Ginger's effect on blood pressure can be traced to its helpful components, which help relax the blood vessels, improving circulation and lowering blood pressure.

Additionally, ginger's anti-inflammatory benefits may add to its blood pressure-lowering powers by avoiding inflammation-induced damage to the circulation system. Incorporating ginger into the diet can be an effective and fun way to harness its health benefits. Fresh ginger can be added to various recipes, from stir-fries to drinks, adding its unique taste and health-promoting qualities. Ginger tea, made with sliced or chopped ginger in hot water, is a soothing beverage that can help digestion and promote relaxation, further supporting cardiovascular health. Ginger pills are available for those needing a more potent form. However, speaking with a healthcare source before starting any new vitamin practice is suggested, especially for people with present health problems or those taking medicine. While ginger offers promising benefits for reducing blood pressure and supporting heart health, it's essential to view it as part of a balanced approach to exercise. A reasonable diet, regular physical exercise, and stress control are critical to heart-healthy life. Ginger can support these practices, giving a natural and delicious way to improve well-being and protect against cardiovascular disease. As we continue to study the possibilities of herbal medicines like ginger, it's clear that these ancient plants are essential for health and healing. By mixing the knowledge of traditional herbalism with modern scientific understanding, we can unlock the full potential of herbs like ginger to support our health and improve our lives.

OLIVE LEAVES: OVERVIEW AND BENEFITS

Olive leaves, drawn from the Olea europaea tree, have been a cornerstone of Mediterranean healing practices for ages, recognized for their health-promoting qualities. These leaves contain a rich mix of antioxidants, most notably oleuropein, which is lauded for its antioxidant, anti-inflammatory, and disease-fighting powers. The mending ability of olive leaves includes a broad range of health benefits, including circulation support, excellent immune function, and better gut health. The circulation effects of olive leaves are particularly noticeable. Oleuropein, the primary substance, has been shown to positively impact heart health by lowering blood pressure, reducing vessel stiffness, and dropping blood fat levels, thereby lessening the risk factors for heart disease. This substance benefits through its antioxidant action, which helps avoid the breakdown of LDL cholesterol, a key reason for atherosclerosis development. Beyond arterial health, olive leaves are antibacterial and helpful against different pathogens, including bacteria, viruses, and fungi. This broad-spectrum antibiotic action is constructive for boosting the immune system and defending against bacterial illnesses. Olive leaves also have an excellent effect on general health. Studies show that oleuropein can improve insulin sensitivity and lower blood sugar levels, aiding it in treating diabetes and metabolic syndrome.

Additionally, the antioxidant qualities of olive leaves help fight reactive stress, a state tied to several chronic diseases, including cancer, Alzheimer's disease, and heart disease. Olive leaves can be added to one's diet by taking olive leaf extract, available in pill or liquid form, or by making tea from dried olive leaves. This allows for a handy and flexible way to harness the health benefits of olive leaves, making them a valuable addition to a balanced health practice focused on natural, plant-based solutions for wellness and energy.

EXPLORING HORSE CHESTNUT: USES AND BENEFITS

Horse Chestnut, officially known as Aesculus hippocastanum, is a tall deciduous tree native to the Balkan Peninsula. With its majestic size, the tree is easily recognizable by its glossy, palmate leaves and distinctive, spiky seed sacks that house the brown, shiny seeds known widely as conkers. Beyond its artistic value, Horse Chestnut has been recognized in plant medicine for its potent health benefits, especially for the blood system. The primary medicinal worth of Horse Chestnut lies in its seeds, bark, and leaves, which contain a substance called aescin. Aescin has been shown to improve the walls of veins and capillaries, promote average blood circulation, and help avoid and treat venous disorders. This condition, marked by swollen legs, varicose veins, and a feeling of heaviness in the limbs, can be significantly eased using Horse Chestnut products. In addition to its circulation benefits, Horse Chestnut shows anti-inflammatory qualities that can reduce swelling and pain linked with recurrent vein failure and haemorrhoids. Its antioxidant components also help protect blood vessels' integrity by removing free radicals and lowering reactive stress, further supporting vascular health. For those looking to add Horse Chestnut into their health practice, it is frequently given as pills, preparations, and skin creams. When using Horse Chestnut goods, it is crucial to stick to the recommended amounts, as excessive usage can lead to side effects such as tiredness, sickness, and stomach pain. As with any plant treatment, speaking with a healthcare source before starting Horse Chestnut is suggested, especially for people on medicine or those with pre-existing health problems. Horse Chestnut's multiple benefits underscore its importance in plant medicine, offering a natural way to improve circulatory health and ease the pain connected with vein illnesses. Its use shows the power of plants to support the body's mending processes, reflecting the spirit of herbalism in supporting general well-being.

HIBISCUS: OVERVIEW AND BENEFITS

Hibiscus, known adequately as Hibiscus sabdariffa, is a flowering plant famous for its bright, giant flowers and healing powers. Originating from warm areas, it has been grown worldwide, not only for its beauty but also for its healing uses. The part of the plant most commonly used for health reasons is the calyx, the protected layer around the flower, which, after drying, is made into a deep-red, tart tea known as hibiscus tea. This plant medicine is packed with antioxidants, including anthocyanins, which give the tea its usual red colour and are known for their health-promoting qualities. Hibiscus tea has been widely used to lower blood pressure. Studies show that the helpful chemicals in hibiscus can help lower systolic and diastolic blood pressure, making it a natural aid for those with hypertension. Its circulation benefits spread to reduce blood fat levels, improving general heart health. Beyond its circulation benefits, hibiscus has diuretic traits that help promote kidney health by increasing pee flow, thereby assisting the body in clearing extra fluids and salts. Its high vitamin C level helps the nervous system, making it an excellent beverage for better health. The anti-inflammatory and antibiotic traits of hibiscus add to its use in treating discomforts and diseases. It's also been used in traditional medicine to support gut and liver health, thanks to its ability to improve digestion and encourage liver cleaning. Incorporating roses into one's food is easy. Hibiscus tea can be enjoyed hot or cold, making it a delicious drink for any season. For those looking to support their health naturally, hibiscus offers a tasty and therapeutic choice, reflecting the spirit of plant medicine's protection and healing power. However, people taking certain drugs, such as hydrochlorothiazide or those with low blood pressure, should speak with a healthcare provider before adding hibiscus to their diet to avoid possible reactions or harmful effects.

TEN HERBAL REMEDIES FOR SUPPORTING HEART HEALTH

Hawthorn Berry Tincture

Beneficial effects

Hawthorn Berry Tincture is praised for its cardiovascular effects, especially in supporting heart health and improving circulation. It has been shown to boost heart muscle activity, lower blood pressure, and improve signs of heart failure. The active substances in hawthorn, including flavonoids and oligomeric procyanidins, add to its antioxidant qualities, which can help lower inflammation and avoid damage to heart cells.

Ingredients

- 1 cup fresh hawthorn berries
- 2 cups vodka or brandy (at least 80 proof)

Instructions

1. Wash the hawthorn berries thoroughly and allow them to dry completely.
2. Once dry, place the berries in a clean, dry jar, filling it up to three-quarters full.
3. Pour the vodka or brandy over the berries, ensuring they are fully covered. Add more alcohol, if necessary, to cover the berries by at least an inch.
4. Seal the jar tightly and mark it with the date and contents.
5. Store the jar in a cool, dark place for 4 to 6 weeks, shaking it gently every few days to mix the contents.
6. After soaking, strain the liquor through a fine mesh strainer or cheesecloth into another clean jar or bottle, pressing the berries to remove as much liquid as possible.
7. Discard the berries and put the squeezed medicine into dark glass dropper bottles for easy use.

Variations

- For a non-alcoholic version, replace the vodka or brandy with apple cider vinegar or glycerin, changing the steeping time as needed. Note that the strength and shelf life may vary with these replacements.
- To improve the heart-supportive qualities, add a few dried rose flowers or a cinnamon stick to the jar during the steeping process.

Storage Tips

Store the Hawthorn Berry Tincture in a cool, dark place. The juice can last several years when appropriately kept in dark glass bottles. Ensure the bottles are tightly sealed to prevent loss and breakdown of the active substances.

Tips for allergens

For those with allergies or responses to booze, the non-alcoholic form offers an acceptable choice. Always start with a small amount to watch for any bad results, especially if you have a history of heart conditions or are taking medicine for heart health, as hawthorn can mix with certain drugs.

Motherwort Tea

Beneficial effects

Motherwort Tea is praised for its heart-supporting benefits, especially its ability to improve heart function and ease heart pains. It works as a light tranquillizer, lowering stress and fear and indirectly benefiting heart health. Additionally, motherwort has long been used to lower high blood pressure, a critical factor in maintaining cardiovascular health.

Ingredients

- 1-2 teaspoons of dried motherwort leaves
- 8 ounces of boiling water
- Honey or lemon (optional, for taste)

Instructions

1. Place the dried motherwort leaves in a tea bag or cup.
2. Pour the hot water over the motherwort leaves.
3. Cover the cup and leave it to sit for 10-15 minutes. The longer it steeps, the stronger the tea will be.
4. Remove the tea sieve or strain the tea to remove the leaves.
5. Add honey or a bit of lemon to improve the taste if desired.
6. Drink the tea once daily, especially in the evening, to utilize its calming benefits for a better night's sleep.

Variations

- For those dealing with stress-induced heart problems, adding a teaspoon of lavender to the tea can improve its cooling effects.
- Combine motherwort with hawthorn berries in the tea to further support blood health.
- For a more complicated taste, include a cinnamon stick or a few slices of fresh ginger in the cup while steeping.

Storage Tips

Put dried motherwort leaves in a covered jar in a cool, dark place to keep their usefulness. Prepared Motherwort Tea is best enjoyed fresh but can be kept in the refrigerator for up to 24 hours. Reheat gently before eating, or enjoy it cold.

Tips for allergens

Individuals with allergies to plants in the Lamiaceae family, which includes motherwort, should continue with caution and may want to speak with a healthcare source before trying this tea. Honey can be removed for those with allergies or veggie tastes; maple syrup can be a plant-based sugar replacement.

Cayenne Pepper Heart Tonic

Beneficial effects

Cayenne Pepper Heart Tonic benefits cardiovascular health by improving blood circulation, lowering blood clots, and dropping blood pressure. Capsaicin, the main ingredient in cayenne pepper, has been shown to have vasodilatory benefits, which can help to widen blood vessels and improve blood flow. This drink can also improve digestion and help in cleaning processes, adding to general heart health.

Ingredients

- One teaspoon of cayenne pepper powder
- Two tablespoons of raw, unfiltered apple cider vinegar
- One tablespoon of raw honey
- 1 cup of warm water

Instructions

1. Mix one teaspoon of cayenne pepper powder in a glass with two tablespoons of raw, unfiltered apple cider vinegar.
2. Add one tablespoon of raw honey to the mix for taste and health benefits.
3. Pour 1 cup of warm water into the glass and stir all the ingredients until they are well mixed and the honey fully dissolves.
4. To improve its circulation benefits, consume this drink once daily, which is best in the morning on an empty stomach.

Variations

- For those sensitive to spice, start with a smaller amount of cayenne pepper powder and gradually increase to the suggested dose as agreed.
- Add a squeeze of fresh lemon juice for extra vitamin C and to improve the taste of the tonic.
- If raw honey is unavailable, replace it with maple syrup for a vegan-friendly choice.

Storage Tips

Prepare the Cayenne Pepper Heart Tonic fresh each morning to ensure strength and effectiveness. It is not recommended to keep the mix as the components are most helpful when devoured after preparation.

Tips for allergens

Individuals with a known allergy to cayenne pepper or other chemicals in the drink should avoid this treatment. As with any food supplement, speaking with a healthcare provider before adding it to your routine is advised, especially for those with present health problems or taking medicine.

Hibiscus Flower Infusion

Beneficial effects

Hibiscus Flower Infusion is praised for its potential to support heart health, thanks to its high vitamin content and ability to help lower blood pressure. Studies show that hibiscus tea can improve blood cholesterol levels and protect against atherosclerosis. Its watery features also increase its usefulness in managing blood pressure, making it a helpful plant treatment for those looking to keep or improve cardiac health.

Ingredients

- Two tablespoons of dried hibiscus flowers
- 8 ounces of boiling water
- Honey or lemon (optional, for taste)

Instructions

1. Place the dried hibiscus flowers in a tea infuser or into a pot.
2. Pour the hot water over the hibiscus flowers.
3. Cover and allow the tea to steep for 5-10 minutes, based on the preferred strength. The longer it steeps, the more influential the taste and healing effects.
4. Strain the tea into a cup, removing the hibiscus flowers.
5. Add honey or a bit of lemon to improve the taste if desired.
6. Enjoy this drink once daily to support heart health.

Variations

- Chill the tea and serve with ice and a piece of mint for a beautiful change.
- Combine with green tea for an extra vitamin boost.
- Add a stick of cinnamon while steeping for extra taste and possibly blood sugar control benefits.

Storage Tips

Dried hibiscus flowers should be stored in a locked jar in a cool, dark place to keep their strength. Prepared Hibiscus Flower Infusion is best served fresh but can be kept in the refrigerator for up to 24 hours. Reheat gently before eating or enjoy cold.

Tips for allergens

Individuals with known intolerance to hibiscus should avoid this blend. Honey can be replaced with maple syrup for those with allergies or veggie tastes.

Garlic and Hawthorn Syrup

Beneficial effects

Garlic and Hawthorn Syrup combines the heart-protective qualities of garlic, known for its ability to lower blood pressure and cholesterol levels, with the cardiovascular benefits of hawthorn, which include improving coronary artery blood flow, reducing heart palpitations, and preventing heart disease. This strong syrup can support heart health, improve circulation, and provide antioxidant protection.

Ingredients

- 1 cup fresh hawthorn berries (or 1/2 cup dried)
- 1/4 cup garlic cloves, peeled and finely chopped
- 2 cups water
- 1 cup honey

Instructions

1. Combine the hawthorn berries, garlic cloves, and water in a medium pot.
2. Bring the mixture to a boil, then reduce the heat and cook for 30 minutes or until the liquid is reduced by half.
3. Strain the mixture through a fine mesh sieve, pressing on the solids to remove as much liquid as possible. Discard the lumps.
4. Return the juice to the pot and add the honey.
5. Warm over low heat, stirring until the honey is fully melted.
6. Remove from heat and allow the syrup to cool.
7. Once cooled, move the syrup to a clean, airtight glass bottle.

Variations

- For a veggie version, replace honey with maple syrup or agave nectar.
- Add a cinnamon stick during cooking for taste and blood sugar control benefits.
- Incorporate a few slices of ginger for its anti-inflammatory benefits and spicy taste.

Storage Tips

Store the Garlic and Hawthorn Syrup in the refrigerator for up to 2 months. Ensure the bottle is tightly shut to keep freshness and strength.

Tips for allergens

Individuals with a garlic allergy should remove this ingredient and increase the amount of hawthorn berries to keep the syrup's heart-supportive effects. Speaking with a healthcare source before use is recommended for those allergic to hawthorn.

Ginkgo Biloba Heart Elixir

Beneficial effects

Ginkgo biloba heart juice benefits cardiovascular health by increasing blood circulation, improving oxygen and food flow to the heart, and offering antioxidant defence against artery damage. Ginkgo biloba has been shown to widen blood vessels, lower blood stiffness, and act as an antioxidant, making it helpful for avoiding and managing heart disease and peripheral artery disease and improving general vascular performance.

Ingredients

- 1/4 cup dried Ginkgo Biloba leaves
- 1 cup water
- One tablespoon honey (optional for sweetness)
- One teaspoon of lemon juice (optional for flavour and added vitamin C)

Instructions

1. Bring 1 cup of water to a boil in a small pot.
2. Add the dried Ginkgo Biloba leaves to the hot water.
3. Reduce the heat and simmer for 10 minutes, allowing the leaves to rest and release their healing chemicals.
4. Remove from heat and strain the mixture to remove the leaves.
5. If wanted, stir in honey and lemon juice to taste.
6. Allow the juice to cool to a comfortable drinking temperature.
7. Consume the Ginkgo Biloba Heart Elixir once daily, best in the morning, to support cardiovascular health throughout the day.

Variations

- Add a teaspoon of dried hawthorn berries to the cooking process for a better heart health mix. Hawthorn is known for its heart-protective traits.
- To support blood pressure control, include a pinch of ground cinnamon in the drink.
- For those who prefer a cold beverage, chill the juice and serve it over ice for a refreshing, heart-healthy drink.

Storage Tips

The Ginkgo Biloba Heart Elixir can be saved in the refrigerator for up to 48 hours. Ensure it's kept in a covered container to maintain strength and taste. Reheat slowly if preferred, but do not boil, as high heat can kill some helpful chemicals.

Tips for allergens

Due to its blood-thinning effects, individuals on blood thinners or those with a past of bleeding problems should speak with a healthcare source before taking Ginkgo biloba. Honey can be removed for those with allergies or diabetes, and lemon juice can be changed with a dash of apple cider vinegar for a different taste profile without losing the health benefits.

Linden Flower Tea

Beneficial effects

Linden Flower Tea is praised for its peaceful and healing qualities, making it an excellent natural cure for stress, anxiety, and sleepiness. Its mild relaxing effect can help relax the nervous system, promote a sense of calm, and help with a restful night's sleep. Additionally, Linden Flower Tea has been known to support heart health by lowering blood pressure and easing stress in the vascular system.

Ingredients

- Two tablespoons of dried linden flowers
- 8 ounces of boiling water
- Honey or lemon (optional, for taste)

Instructions

1. Place the dried linden flowers in a tea bag or cup.
2. Pour the hot water over the linden leaves.
3. Cover the cup and leave it to sit for 10-15 minutes. This causes the linden leaves' healing powers to be fully released.
4. Remove the tea strainer or strain the tea to remove the extra flowers.
5. Add honey or a bit of lemon to improve the taste if desired.
6. Enjoy the tea warm, especially in the evening, to boost its peaceful and heart health benefits.

Variations

- For extra calm effects, add a teaspoon of chamomile to the brew.
- To improve the taste and health benefits, include a cinnamon stick or a few slices of fresh ginger in the cup while steeping.

Storage Tips

Store empty dried linden leaves in a covered jar in a cool, dark place to maintain their usefulness. Prepared Linden Flower Tea is best served fresh but can be kept in the refrigerator for up to 24 hours. Reheat gently before eating.

Tips for allergens

Individuals with allergies to plants in the Tilia family should continue carefully and may want to speak with a healthcare source before trying Linden Flower Tea. Honey can be removed for those with allergies or veggie tastes; maple syrup can be a plant-based sugar replacement.

Turmeric and Ginger Heart Health Drink

Beneficial effects

The Turmeric and Ginger Heart Health Drink is a potent mix made to support blood health. With its main ingredient, curcumin, turmeric has anti-inflammatory and protective traits that can help lower the risk of heart disease. Similarly, ginger adds to the heart's health by improving blood circulation and cutting cholesterol levels. Together, they make a strong drink that supports heart health, boosts the immune system, and lowers inflammation.

Ingredients

- One teaspoon of turmeric powder
- One teaspoon of grated ginger
- One tablespoon of honey (optional for sweetness)
- 1 cup of water
- Juice of half a lemon

Instructions

1. Bring 1 cup of water to a boil in a small pot.
2. Add the chopped ginger and turmeric powder to the hot water.
3. Reduce the heat and let it cook for about 10 minutes.
4. Remove from heat and strain the mixture into a mug.
5. Add half a lemon juice to the mug.
6. Stir in honey to taste, if desired.
7. Enjoy the drink warm; it is best on an empty stomach in the morning for maximum benefits.

Variations

- Add a pinch of chilli pepper to the drink for an extra circulation boost. Cayenne pepper is known for improving blood flow and lowering blood pressure.
- Replace water with green tea for an extra vitamin kick.
- For those who prefer a cold beverage, leave the drink to cool and add ice cubes for a delicious turmeric and ginger iced tea.

Storage Tips

It's best to make the Turmeric and Ginger Heart Health Drink fresh for each use to ensure the strength of its active ingredients. However, if you need to make it in advance, store it in a tight jar in the refrigerator for up to 24 hours. Reheat gently before eating, or enjoy it cold.

Tips for allergens

Individuals with allergies to turmeric or ginger should start with a small amount to ensure no harmful effects occur. Honey can be removed for those with allergies or food preferences, and lemon juice can be changed according to taste and tolerance.

Cinnamon and Hawthorn Berry Decoction

Beneficial effects

Cinnamon and Hawthorn Berry Decoction is a heart-healthy plant medicine known for its ability to support cardiovascular health. Cinnamon is praised for its protective qualities, which can help lower blood pressure and cholesterol levels. At the same time, hawthorn berry is respected for its ability to strengthen the heart, improve circulation, and steady the beating. Together, they form a potent mixture that can aid in avoiding heart disease and improving general heart health.

Ingredients

- One tablespoon of dried hawthorn berries
- One cinnamon stick
- 2 cups of water
- Honey (optional, to taste)

Instructions

1. Combine the dried hawthorn berries, cinnamon sticks, and water in a small pot.
2. Bring the mixture to a boil, then drop the heat and cook for 20 minutes. This allows the active chemicals in the hawthorn berries and cinnamon to be released into the water.
3. Remove from heat and strain the juice into a cup, removing the hawthorn berries and cinnamon stick.
4. If wanted, add honey to taste for sweetness.
5. To support heart health, drink the mixture warm, ideally once in the morning and once in the evening.

Variations

- Allow the mixture to cook for 10 minutes before dividing it into a more substantial pot.
- Add a slice of fresh ginger during cooking for extra anti-inflammatory benefits.
- Mix with a splash of lemon juice before serving for an extra boost of vitamin C and a delicious taste.

Storage Tips

The Cinnamon and Hawthorn Berry Decoction is best eaten fresh but can be saved in the refrigerator for up to 48 hours. Reheat gently before eating, or enjoy it cold.

Tips for allergens

Individuals with a known response to hawthorn should avoid this tea. Honey can be changed with maple syrup for those with allergies or veggie tastes.

Rosemary and Lemon Balm Heart Support Tea

Beneficial effects

Rosemary and Lemon Balm Heart Improve Tea is a natural treatment to improve blood health. Rosemary is known for its antioxidant qualities, which can help improve blood circulation and strengthen heart function. On the other hand, lemon balm has a cooling effect on the body, lowering stress and anxiety, which are known risk factors for heart disease. Together, they form a heart-healthy tea that can aid in dropping blood pressure, reducing heartbeats, and improving general heart health.

Ingredients

- One teaspoon of dried rosemary
- One teaspoon of dried lemon balm leaves
- 8 ounces of boiling water
- Honey (optional, for taste)

Instructions

1. Place the dried rosemary and lemon balm leaves in a tea bag or straight into a cup.
2. Pour the hot water over the herbs.
3. Cover the cup and let it sit for 10-15 minutes. This allows the herbs' healing powers to be fully released.
4. Remove the tea strainer or strain the tea to remove the extra herbs.
5. If wanted, add honey to taste.
6. Enjoy this tea once daily to help heart health.

Variations

- For a refreshing twist, add a slice of fresh lemon or a few fresh mint leaves to the tea while it steeps.
- Combine with hibiscus flowers for extra blood pressure-lowering effects.
- For a stronger tea, increase the steeping time to 20 minutes or add an extra teaspoon of each herb.

Storage Tips

Store extra dried rosemary and lemon balm leaves in covered containers in a cool, dark place to keep their strength. Prepared tea is best served fresh but can be kept in the refrigerator for up to 24 hours. Reheat gently before eating, or enjoy it cold as an iced tea.

Tips for allergens

Individuals with allergies to plants in the Lamiaceae family, including rosemary and lemon balm, should continue carefully and may want to speak with a healthcare source before trying this tea. Honey can be removed for those with allergies or veggie tastes; plant-based sugar can be used as a choice.

HERBS FOR FEMALE AND MALE HEALTH

In handling the complex world of herbs for female and male health, it's important to understand the unique hormonal and chemical differences that require personalized herbal treatments. Specific herbs to support and improve female and male health have been a cornerstone of traditional medicine across different countries for ages. These plants naturally balance hormones, improve pregnancy, and treat specific gender-related health problems. For women, plants such as Chasteberry (Vitex agnus-castus) have been respected for their ability to control monthly cycles and ease signs of premenstrual syndrome (PMS). Chasteberry's effect on the pituitary gland helps control female hormones, which can be helpful for those dealing with unpredictable periods or pregnancy troubles. The Red Raspberry Leaf (Rubus idaeus) is another veggie praised for its relaxing uterine qualities, often suggested during pregnancy to support uterus health. However, its use should be reviewed with a healthcare expert. On the other hand, male health has been traditionally supported by herbs like Saw Palmetto (Serenoa repens), which has been studied for its effectiveness in improving symptoms of benign prostatic hyperplasia (BPH) and its potential impacts on hair loss due to its ability to inhibit 5-alpha-reductase, an enzyme involved in the conversion of testosterone to dihydrotestosterone (DHT). With its adaptogenic traits, Ginseng (Panax ginseng) has been used to boost physical performance, support energy, and improve sexual dysfunction by supporting nitric oxide production in the walls of blood vessels. Both genders can benefit from adaptogenic plants such as Ashwagandha (Withania somnifera), which helps handle stress and improve general health by controlling the body's reaction to stress and balancing adrenal hormones. This is especially important as stress can greatly impact both female and male reproductive health by changing chemicals like cortisol and testosterone. Incorporating these herbs into daily routines requires understanding their qualities, amounts, and possible mixtures with other drugs. For instance, while Chasteberry may be helpful for premenstrual conditions, it might mix with artificial contraception, possibly lowering its usefulness. Similarly, while Saw Palmetto is generally considered safe, it may mix with blood-thinning meds and should be used with care. Using plants for health is thorough, stressing the healing of symptoms and the development of general well-being. This includes a healthy diet, regular physical exercise, mental methods, and plant nutrients. As we dig deeper into the details of herbal treatments for female and male health, it becomes clear that the knowledge of old herbalism, mixed with current scientific thinking, offers strong tools for handling gender-specific health needs. Expanding upon the basis of herbal support for female and male health, additional herbs like Dong Quai (Angelica sinensis) and Tribulus Terrestris are key elements in this natural arsenal. Dong Quai, often called the "female ginseng," is praised for strengthening blood, increasing circulation, and controlling the monthly cycle, making it a cornerstone in traditional Chinese medicine for women's health. Its phytoestrogen components offer a normal effect on estrogen levels, helping in the relief of menopause signs and monthly problems. However, due to its strong effects, Dong Quai should be used under the direction of a healthcare worker, especially for those on blood thinners or hormone-related medicines. Tribulus Terrestris, on the other hand, has gained respect for its role in male health, especially in improving desire and sexual function. Studies show that Tribulus may raise amounts of luteinizing hormone, which tells the body to make more testosterone, a key hormone in male reproductive and sexual health. This herb's adaptogenic traits also support general stamina and energy levels, making it a valuable product for both genders but especially helpful for men looking to improve their sexual health and performance. Red Clover (Trifolium pratense) is another plant that helps both female and male health. Rich in isoflavones, a type of phytoestrogen, Red Clover can help handle menopause symptoms, such as hot flashes and night sweats in women, while also giving circulation benefits by improving blood flow and lowering cholesterol levels. Its role in prostate health is also important, with some proof showing that Red Clover may help lower the chance of benign prostatic hyperplasia and prostate cancer. Maca (Lepidium meyenii) is a Peruvian herb known for its hormone-balancing benefits and energy-boosting traits. For women, Maca can ease signs of menopause, including mood changes and sleep problems, while for men, it has been shown to improve sperm production and movement, as well as boost libido. Maca's adaptogenic traits make it an excellent vitamin for fighting stress and tiredness, adding to general well-being and energy. Black Cohosh (Actaea racemosa) has been widely used for easing menopausal symptoms, such as hot flashes, mood swings, and sleep problems. Its success is linked to its ability to mimic the effects of estrogen in the body, making it a popular choice for women going through menopause. However, Black Cohosh should be treated with care, as it may mix with certain drugs and is not suggested for people with liver problems. Incorporating these herbs into one's health practice offers a broad approach to treating specific female and male health concerns, from hormonal changes and reproductive problems to stress and age. To ensure safety and efficiency, speaking with a healthcare source before starting any plant product is crucial, especially for people with current health problems or those taking other medicines. By mixing the knowledge of old herbalism with current science studies, people can tap the power of nature to support their health and well-being, reflecting the spirit of total medicine and preventive care.

CHASTEBERRY: OVERVIEW AND BENEFITS

Chasteberry, officially known as Vitex agnus-castus, is a herb famous for controlling hormonal changes, especially in women. Originating from the Mediterranean area and parts of Asia, this plant has been used in ancient health methods for thousands of years. The chasteberry tree offers small, sweet berries that, once dried, can be used to prepare preparations, drinks, and pills. These goods exploit the power of chasteberry's active ingredients, which include flavonoids, iridoid glycosides, and essential oils, adding to its therapeutic benefits. The main advantage of chaste berry lies in its unique ability to fix the balance of female hormones. It slightly affects the pituitary gland, the body's primary hormone stabilizer, which changes amounts of luteinizing hormone, follicle-stimulating hormone, and prolactin. This chemical control is beneficial for women suffering from premenstrual syndrome (PMS), period problems, and pregnancy issues. By creating a better hormonal environment, chaste nuts can ease symptoms such as mood swings, breast soreness, and unpredictable cycles.

Moreover, chaste berries have been studied for their role in controlling symptoms linked with menopause and polycystic ovary syndrome (PCOS), giving a natural choice or addition to standard hormone treatments. Its ability to lower high prolactin levels makes it a valuable plant for women dealing with breastfeeding problems or prolactinoma, a type of average pituitary growth. While chasteberry is generally considered safe for most individuals, it is crucial to speak with a healthcare provider before adding it to your health plan, especially for those on hormonal drugs or with hormone-sensitive conditions. Integrating chaste berries into daily life through drinks, pills, or preparations represents a complete approach to wellness, stressing the value of natural, plant-based solutions in keeping reproductive health and general well-being.

RED RASPBERRY ESSENTIALS

Red Raspberry, officially known as Rubus idaeus, is a plant that is as flexible as it is helpful, with its roots deeply rooted in the tales of herbal medicine across different countries. This annual plant, native to Europe and parts of Asia, is defined by its woody stems, green leaves, and the famous red raspberries it bears, which have been eaten and utilized for their medical qualities for ages. The leaves of the red raspberry plant, often ignored by the fame of the fruit, hold a treasure trove of health benefits and have been widely used in herbal teas and medicines. The leaves of the red raspberry plant are rich in vitamins and minerals, including Vitamin C, magnesium, potassium, iron, and b-vitamins, making them a nutritional powerhouse. They are also rich in antioxidants that fight oxidative stress and reduce inflammation. One of the most popular uses of red raspberry leaves is in women's health, especially during pregnancy. The leaves are thought to strengthen the uterus walls and muscles, which can lead to a faster and easier birth.

Moreover, red raspberry leaf tea is often recommended to ease menstrual pain and control cycles because it can tone the pelvic muscles and balance hormones. Beyond its uses in women's health, red raspberry leaves have been used to soothe stomach pain. Their anti-inflammatory features can help in healing conditions such as diarrhoea and gastritis, calming the stomach and guts. Additionally, the acidic qualities of the leaves make them effective in tightening and shaping tissues, further helping treat minor cuts, burns, and skin irritations when applied directly. The benefits of red raspberry stretch to its ability to control blood sugar levels, making it a subject of interest for people with diabetes. The leaves contain tannins and flavonoids, which are thought to help improve insulin sensitivity and, thus, reduce blood sugar.

Furthermore, the circulatory benefits of red raspberry leaves should be noticed. The potassium in the leaves adds to heart health by helping control blood pressure and lowering hypertension risk. Incorporating red raspberry leaves into one's diet or exercise routine can be as easy as making tea from dried leaves, a traditional and effective way to access their health benefits. For those looking to harness the external benefits, making drinks or poultices from the leaves for direct application to the skin can provide healing relief for different skin conditions. Despite the multiple benefits, it is essential for people, especially pregnant women, to speak with a healthcare provider before adding red raspberry leaves into their diet to ensure they are proper for their unique health circumstances. As with any natural treatment, balance is critical, and knowing the possible combos with other drugs is essential for safe use. Red raspberry leaves stand as a testament to the power of plants in supporting health and happiness, representing the principles of old herbalism in giving natural, time-tested answers for modern life. Their wide range of benefits, from women's health support to anti-inflammatory and stomach-soothing qualities, make them a valuable addition to the plant medicine cabinet, continuing the history of natural healing practices for future generations.

DONG QUAI BENEFITS FOR MALE HEALTH

Dong Quai, officially known as Angelica sinensis, is a treasured herb in Traditional Chinese Medicine, often dubbed as "female ginseng" for its benefits in women's health. However, its benefits stretch to male health, solving problems like blood health and inflammation. Dong Quai's root is the part utilized for medical reasons, having substances such as ferulic acid, which works as an anti-inflammatory and antioxidant. Dong Quai offers several health benefits for guys, including the growth of blood health, better circulation, and support for a healthy heart. These benefits are vital, considering vascular health is a significant worry for many guys, especially as they age. The anti-inflammatory features of Dong Quai make it helpful in lowering the risk of prostate issues and other inflammation conditions that can affect men's health.

Additionally, its part in supporting blood circulation can help support male sexual health, improving general strength and energy levels. While Dong Quai is widely known for its benefits in female reproductive health, its circulatory and anti-inflammatory benefits are usually relevant, making it a valuable herb in male health tools. When adding Dong Quai into a health program, it's essential to speak with a healthcare provider, especially for people on blood thinners or those with hormone-sensitive conditions, to ensure its fit and safety. Dong Quai can be taken in various forms, including pills, drinks, and teas, giving freedom in how it can be combined into daily habits. Its use, while helpful, should be dealt with with an understanding of its strong effects and possible clashes with other drugs. Through wise use, Dong Quai can be a powerful component of a complete approach to male health, supporting cardiovascular well-being, lowering inflammation, and improving general energy.

GINSENG: OVERVIEW AND BENEFITS

Ginseng, taken from the root of plants in the genus Panax, is a cornerstone in traditional Chinese medicine, especially in Asian countries. Recognized for its thick roots, this annual plant is respected for its healing qualities and has been utilized for millennia. Panax ginseng, often referred to as Korean ginseng, represents the quintessence of energy and is defined by its ginsenosides, which are unique chemicals critical to its health benefits. Ginseng's benefits include improved physical and mental ability, immune system support, and better blood sugar control. Its adaptogenic traits, capable of helping the body survive stress, make it a helpful partner in today's fast-paced world. Ginseng is charged with anti-inflammatory and antioxidant actions, adding to its ability to lower the risk of chronic diseases. For brain function, ginseng has shown promise in improving memory and attention, making it a subject of interest for older groups and those wanting mental clarity. Its part in immunity improvement is underscored by its ability to increase the body's defences against sickness.

Additionally, ginseng's effect on blood sugar levels has gained interest for its possible benefits in controlling diabetes. In the world of physical strength, ginseng is often sought by players and people trying to improve their energy levels and physical ability. Its ability to reduce sleepiness benefits those facing energy slumps or constant tiredness. While ginseng's benefits are appealing, it is crucial to approach its use with understanding, especially regarding amount and time, to maximize its healing potential while lowering harmful effects. Consulting with a healthcare provider before adding ginseng into one's routine ensures a personalized approach that considers individual health needs and possible drug responses. In taking ginseng, people tap into an old energy source, utilizing its adaptogenic and healing properties to support general well-being. Its valued place in plant medicine continues to be supported by traditional practices and modern scientific study, filling the gap between old knowledge and current health interests.

EXPLORING TRIBULUS TERRESTRIS: USES AND BENEFITS

Tribulus Terrestris, widely known as puncture vine, has been a staple in traditional medicine across various countries for ages, especially in areas like the Mediterranean, India, and China. This plant is known for its spiny fruit, which is the source of its medicinal qualities. The active substances within Tribulus Terrestris, including saponins, flavonoids, and alkaloids, add to its health benefits, making it a sought-after product in the world of natural wellness. Tribulus Terrestris's benefits range from better sexual health to enhanced sports ability. In men, it is most famous for its ability to naturally raise amounts of luteinizing hormone, which tells the body to increase testosterone production. This finding is beneficial for boosting libido, better sperm movement, and general sexual health.

Additionally, the adaptogenic traits of Tribulus Terrestris help increase the body's response to stress and raise energy levels, making it a popular vitamin among athletes and those looking to improve physical performance and endurance. For women, Tribulus Terrestris offers benefits in hormone control and pregnancy improvement. Creating a healthier endocrine environment can ease signs of premenstrual syndrome and menopause, adding to general well-being. Beyond its sexual and performance-enhancing effects, Tribulus Terrestris is also linked with circulation benefits. It aids in keeping healthy blood pressure levels and supports heart health, thanks to its vasodilatory effects. Its part in supporting healthy cholesterol levels further underscores its circulation benefits. Despite its wide range of health benefits, people need to speak with a healthcare provider before putting Tribulus Terrestris into their diet, especially those with hormone-sensitive conditions or those taking medicines. Understanding the right amount and available combos is essential for getting the benefits of Tribulus Terrestris while ensuring safety and success.

EXPLORING SAW PALMETTO: USES & BENEFITS

Saw Palmetto, officially known as Serenoa repens, is a small palm tree native to the southeastern United States. Its leaves are highly respected for their healing powers, especially in treating benign prostatic hyperplasia (BPH), a problem affecting the prostate gland in men. The active chemicals within saw palmetto leaves, including fatty acids and phytosterols, are thought to stop the enzyme 5-alpha-reductase. This enzyme turns testosterone into dihydrotestosterone (DHT), a hormone involved with prostate growth and hair loss. By interfering with this process, saw Palmetto may help lessen the signs of BPH, such as urine frequency and nighttime peeing, and may also slow hair loss. Beyond its uses in prostate health and hair loss, saw Palmetto has been studied for its anti-inflammatory properties, making it a possible aid in treating chronic pelvic pain syndrome and other inflammatory conditions. Its ability to stop the change of testosterone to DHT may also make it helpful for women having polycystic ovary syndrome (PCOS), a disease marked by extra DHT. While saw Palmetto is generally considered safe, it's essential to speak with a healthcare provider before starting any new vitamin, especially for people taking drugs for blood clots or hormone-related treatments. Saw Palmetto can be taken in various forms, including pills, tablets, and liquid extracts, giving freedom to combine into a healthy habit. Its use demonstrates the value of natural, plant-based solutions in handling health problems and meeting the goals of general well-being and prevention care.

TEN HERBAL REMEDIES FOR FEMALE AND MALE HEALTH

Dong Quai Tonic

Beneficial effects

Dong Quai Tonic is recognized for its ability to control hormones and improve sexual health in both women and men. In women, it is known to ease monthly cramps, control menstrual cycles, and treat menopause symptoms. For men, Dong Quai helps improve sperm quality and promotes general energy. Its anti-inflammatory and antioxidant benefits support circulatory health, making it helpful for heart function and circulation.

Ingredients

- 1/4 cup dried Dong Quai root
- 1 litre of water
- Honey or lemon (optional, for taste)

Instructions

1. Place the dried Dong Quai root in a big pot.
2. Add 1 litre of water to the pot and bring to a boil.
3. Once boiling, drop the heat and cook for 30 to 40 minutes, allowing the Dong Quai to taste the water.
4. After boiling, strain the drink to remove the Dong Quai root pieces, putting the juice into a clean container.
5. If wanted, add honey or lemon to taste.
6. Consume one cup of the Dong Quai drink every day, best in the morning, to reap its full benefits throughout the day.

Variations

- For extra benefits, include a slice of fresh ginger or a cinnamon stick during the cooking process to improve the tonic's warming qualities.
- Combine with red raspberry leaf tea for extra sexual health support in females.
- For a relaxed effect, especially helpful during hot months, leave the drink to cool and chill before eating.

Storage Tips

The Dong Quai Tonic can be stored in the refrigerator for up to 5 days. To maintain its strength and taste, it should be kept in a covered container. Reheat gently before eating, or enjoy it cold.

Tips for allergens

Individuals with known plant allergens, especially members of the Apiaceae family, should approach Dong Quai cautiously and may want to speak with a healthcare source before eating it. Honey can be changed with maple syrup for those with allergies or veggie tastes.

Saw Palmetto Tea

Beneficial effects

Saw Palmetto Tea is known for its ability to support male health, especially in treating and preventing benign prostatic hyperplasia (BPH) and hair loss. It works by stopping the enzyme 5-alpha-reductase, which turns testosterone into dihydrotestosterone (DHT), a hormone involved with prostate growth and hair loss. Regular drinking can help lower bladder symptoms linked with BPH, such as frequent peeing and trouble urinating, and may also contribute to hair sprouting.

Ingredients

- One teaspoon of dried saw palmetto berries
- 8 ounces of boiling water
- Honey or lemon (optional, for taste)

Instructions

1. Crush the dried saw palmetto berries using a blender and pestle to release their active chemicals.
2. Place the crushed berries in a tea bag or right into a cup.
3. Pour the hot water over the saw palmetto nuts.
4. Cover the cup and leave it to sit for 10-15 minutes.
5. Remove the tea strainer or strain the tea to remove the berries.
6. Add honey or a bit of lemon to improve the taste if desired.
7. Drink the tea once daily, best in the evening, to support man's health.

Variations

- Mix saw Palmetto with nettle leaf tea for extra benefits, further supporting prostate health and lowering signs of BPH.
- Include a cinnamon stick while steeping to add a spicy taste and extra anti-inflammatory benefits.
- For those looking to support hair growth, mix in a few drops of pumpkin seed oil after steeping, as it is also known to inhibit DHT.

Storage Tips

Store dried saw palmetto berries in a locked jar in a cool, dark place to protect their strength. Prepared Saw Palmetto Tea is best served fresh but can be kept in the refrigerator for up to 24 hours. Reheat gently before eating, or enjoy it cold.

Tips for allergens

Individuals with plant allergies in the palm family should continue carefully and may want to speak with a healthcare source before trying to see palmetto tea. Honey and lemon can be removed for those with allergies or food restrictions.

Red Clover Infusion

Beneficial effects

Red Clover Infusion is known for its ability to support female and male health, especially in balancing hormone levels and improving general sexual health. For women, it can help ease signs of menopause, such as hot flashes and night sweats, due to its phytoestrogen content. For men, it may help in prostate health and lower the risk of prostate problems. Additionally, its anti-inflammatory benefits make it helpful for cardiovascular health, improving circulation and possibly reducing the risk of heart disease.

Ingredients

- 1-2 teaspoons dried red clover flowers
- 8 ounces of boiling water
- Honey or lemon (optional, for taste)

Instructions

1. Place the dried red clover leaves in a tea bag or cup.
2. Pour the hot water over the red clover leaves.
3. Cover the cup and let it sit for 15-20 minutes. This allows the red clover to fully release its helpful traits.
4. Remove the tea strainer or strain the tea to remove the extra flowers.
5. Add honey or a bit of lemon to improve the taste if desired.
6. Drink the mixture once or twice daily to support hormonal balance and sexual health.

Variations

- Mix in a teaspoon of dandelion root or leaves for added cleaning benefits during the steeping process.
- Combine with peppermint leaves for a refreshing taste and extra gut support.
- Add a teaspoon of chamomile leaves to support skin health, improving the infusion's anti-inflammatory benefits.

Storage Tips

Store unused dried red clover flowers in a covered jar in a cool, dark place to keep their usefulness. Prepared Red Clover Infusion is best served fresh but can be kept in the refrigerator for up to 24 hours. Reheat gently before eating, or enjoy it cold.

Tips for allergens

Due to its phytoestrogen content, people with a past of hormone-sensitive conditions should speak with a healthcare source before eating red clover. Honey can be changed with maple syrup for those with allergies or veggie tastes.

Black Cohosh Root Decoction

Beneficial effects

Black Cohosh Root Decoction is widely used to support female health, especially in easing symptoms linked with menopause, such as hot flashes, mood swings, and sleep problems. Its phytoestrogenic traits may help balance hormone levels, giving relief from menopause symptoms. Additionally, black cohosh has been used to ease menstrual pain and to support sexual health.

Ingredients

- One teaspoon of dried black cohosh root
- 1 cup water

Instructions

1. Add one teaspoon of dried black cohosh root to a pot.
2. Pour 1 cup of water over the black cohosh root.
3. Bring the mixture to a boil, then drop the heat and cook for 20-30 minutes.
4. Strain the juice into a cup, removing the black cohosh root.
5. Allow the soup to cool to a comfortable drinking temperature before eating.
6. Drink 1 cup once daily, best in the morning, to watch for any harmful effects throughout the day.

Variations

- For extra benefits, mix with herbs such as red clover or dong quai, known for their helpful role in female health.
- To improve the taste, add a natural sugar such as honey or a slice of lemon.

Storage Tips

Prepare the Black Cohosh Root Decoction fresh for each use to ensure the best efficiency. It is not recommended to keep the juice for later use, as the active chemicals may degrade over time.

Tips for allergens

Individuals with allergies to plants in the Ranunculaceae family, which includes black cohosh, should continue with caution and speak with a healthcare source before trying this treatment.

Maca Root Elixir

Beneficial effects

Maca Root Elixir is famous for its ability to boost energy, strength, and mood, making it particularly helpful for both female and male health. It supports hormonal balance, improves sexual health, and boosts pregnancy. Rich in vitamins, minerals, and phytonutrients, maca root can also increase the immune system and enhance energy, making it a powerful tonic for general well-being.

Ingredients

- One tablespoon of organic maca root powder
- 1 cup of almond milk or water
- One teaspoon of honey or maple syrup (optional for sweetness)
- A pinch of cinnamon (optional for flavour)

Instructions

1. Warm the almond milk or water in a small pot over medium heat until it is just about to boil, but do not boil.
2. Add the maca root powder to the warm liquid and mix until the maca powder is fully dissolved.
3. Remove from heat and stir in the honey or maple syrup and a pinch of cinnamon, if using, until well mixed.
4. Pour the beverage into a mug.
5. Enjoy the maca root tea warm. It is best in the morning to kickstart your day or before physical exercise for an energy boost.

Variations

- For a cold version, mix the maca root powder with cold almond milk or water and ice cubes in a blender for a delicious drink.
- Add a teaspoon of chocolate powder to make a sweet version of the maca root beverage, improving its mood-boosting properties.
- Incorporate a half teaspoon of vanilla extract for a taste of sweetness and aroma without additional sweets.

Storage

Tips

To ensure maximum strength and benefits, it is best to make the maca root elixir fresh for each use. However, if you need to make it in advance, store it in a tight jar in the refrigerator for up to 24 hours. Shake or mix well before drinking.

Tips for allergens

For nut allergies, switch almond milk with oats, rice, or other non-nut milk choices. If you have honey issues, maple syrup is an excellent vegan-friendly sugar choice.

Chasteberry Tea

Beneficial effects

Chasteberry Tea, made from the fruit of the chaste tree, has long been used to support female health, especially in controlling monthly cycles and easing symptoms of premenstrual syndrome (PMS). It is thought to work on the pituitary gland to balance hormone levels, possibly easing breast soreness, mood swings, and other PMS symptoms. Additionally, chaste berries may support male health by promoting prostate health and balancing testosterone levels.

Ingredients

- One teaspoon of dried chaste berry (Vitex agnus-castus)
- 8 ounces of boiling water
- Honey or lemon (optional, for taste)

Instructions

1. Place the dried chasteberry in a tea bag or right into a cup.
2. Pour the hot water over the chaste berry.
3. Cover the cup and leave it to sit for 10-15 minutes. This steeping time helps the healing chemicals from the chaste berry to be released.
4. Remove the tea strainer or strain the tea to remove the chaste berry bits.
5. Add honey or a bit of lemon to improve the taste if desired.
6. Drink the tea once daily, best in the morning, to support hormonal balance and ease signs of hormonal imbalances.

Variations

- For extra hormonal support, mix chaste berry tea with other hormone-balancing herbs, such as red raspberry leaf or dandelion root.
- To improve the relaxing effects and further ease PMS symptoms, add a teaspoon of dried lavender or chamomile to the tea while steeping.
- Allow the tea to cool and chill for a nice cold tea version. Serve over ice with a slice of lemon.

Storage Tips

Put dried chaste berries in a covered jar in a cool, dark place to keep their usefulness. Prepared Chasteberry Tea is best served fresh but can be kept in the refrigerator for up to 24 hours. Reheat gently before eating, or enjoy it cold.

Tips for allergens

Individuals with a past of hormone-sensitive conditions should speak with a healthcare source before drinking chaste berry tea. Honey can be removed for those with allergies or veggie tastes; plant-based sugar can be used as a choice.

Nettle Leaf Infusion

Beneficial effects

Nettle Leaf Infusion is famous for its rich mineral content, including iron, magnesium, and silica, making it an excellent tonic for blood health, hair, skin, and nails. Its watery features help flush toxins from the body, supporting kidney and urine tract health. Additionally, nettle has anti-inflammatory qualities that can ease signs of gout and allergies, and its natural antibiotic properties make it helpful for those suffering from seasonal allergies.

Ingredients

- One tablespoon of dried nettle leaves
- 8 ounces of boiling water
- Honey or lemon (optional, for taste)

Instructions

1. Place the dried nettle leaves in a tea bag or cup.
2. Pour the hot water over the nettle leaves.
3. Cover the cup and leave it to sit for 10-15 minutes. This causes the nettle's healing powers to be fully released.
4. Remove the tea strainer or strain the tea to remove the extra leaves.
5. Add honey or a bit of lemon to improve the taste if desired.
6. Enjoy the mixture warmly once in the morning and once in the evening to maximize its health benefits.

Variations

- For extra cleaning effects, include a slice of fresh ginger or a dash of cinnamon while steeping.
- Combine with peppermint leaves for a refreshing taste and extra gut support.
- Leave the mix to cool and chill for a nice summer drink. Serve over ice with a sprig of fresh mint.

Storage Tips

Store unused dried nettle leaves in a covered jar in a cool, dark place to protect their usefulness. Prepared Nettle Leaf Infusion is best enjoyed fresh but can be kept in the refrigerator for up to 24 hours. Reheat gently before eating, or enjoy it cold.

Tips for allergens

Individuals with known sensitivities to nettle should start with a small amount to ensure no harmful effects appear. Honey can be removed for those with allergies or food preferences, and lemon juice can be changed according to taste and tolerance.

Shatavari Root Tonic

Beneficial effects

Shatavari Root Tonic is recognized in Ayurvedic medicine for supporting female and male health, significantly improving pregnancy and reproductive health. It is known for its adaptogenic traits, helping to control and balance hormones, support the immune system, and lower stress. For women, Shatavari helps ease period cramps and handle signs of PMS and menopause. For men, it can boost energy and support healthy sperm production.

Ingredients

- One tablespoon of dried Shatavari root powder
- 1 cup water
- Honey or maple syrup (optional, for taste)

Instructions

1. Bring 1 cup of water to a boil in a small pot.
2. Add one tablespoon of dried Shatavari root powder to the hot water.
3. Reduce the heat and simmer for 10 minutes, allowing the Shatavari to taste the water.
4. Strain the tonic into a cup, removing the solid bits.
5. If wanted, sweeten with honey or maple syrup to taste.
6. Consume the Shatavari Root Tonic once daily, which is best in the morning, to gain full benefits throughout the day.

Variations

- Add a pinch of ground cinnamon or cardamom to improve the tonic's healing effects during cooking.
- Mix the drained juice with a small banana or a handful of veggies before eating to boost vitamins and minerals.
- For those looking for a cooling effect, especially in hot countries or seasons, leave the drink to cool and serve it cold.

Storage Tips

Please don't open the dried Shatavari root powder jar until it is ready to use. Store it in a cool, dark place. You can keep the drink in the fridge for up to 24 hours, but it tastes best when you drink it right away. It would help if you kept it in a clean, sealed box.

Tips for allergens

Since Shatavari comes from the same family as asparagus, people who are allergic to it should be careful and might want to talk to a doctor before adding it to their diet. People allergic to sugar can leave out honey and maple syrup or replace them with a different product that fits their needs.

Tribulus Terrestris Tea

Beneficial effects

Tribulus Terrestris Tea is well-known for giving people more energy and helping both men's and women's health. Many people have used it to boost desire, improve sexual performance, and protect the reproductive system. It is also thought to help keep hormones in order and give people more power and energy. This makes Tribulus Terrestris a valuable plant for improving overall health.

Ingredients

- 1-2 teaspoons of dried Tribulus Terrestris fruit
- 8 ounces of boiling water
- Honey or lemon (optional, for taste)

Instructions

1. Use a tea infuser or put the dried Tribulus Terrestris fruit in a cup.
2. The water should be poured over the Tribulus Terrestris.
3. Cover the cup and let it sit for 10-15 minutes. This allows the plant's active chemicals to be released into the water.
4. Remove the tea strainer or strain the tea to remove the dried fruit.
5. Add honey or a bit of lemon to improve the taste if desired.
6. Enjoy this tea once or twice daily, best in the morning or early afternoon, to support energy and health.

Variations

- For a more involved taste, add a cinnamon stick or a few slices of fresh ginger to the cup while steeping.
- Combine with ginseng tea for an extra energy boost.
- Allow the tea to cool and chill for those wanting a cold brew. Serve over ice for a relaxing drink.

Storage Tips

Store unsold dried Tribulus Terrestris fruit in a locked jar in a cool, dark place to protect its usefulness. Prepared Tribulus Terrestris Tea is best enjoyed fresh but can be kept in the refrigerator for up to 24 hours. Reheat gently before eating, or enjoy it cold.

Tips for allergens

Individuals with reactions to plants in the Zygophyllaceae family should continue carefully and may want to speak with a healthcare source before trying Tribulus Terrestris Tea. Honey can be removed for those with allergies or veggie tastes; plant-based sugar can be used as a choice.

Damiana Leaf Infusion

Beneficial effects

Damiana Leaf Infusion is famous for improving happiness, lowering stress, and boosting sexual health in both men and women. It works as a weak antidepressant, helping to ease nervousness and promote a sense of well-being. Additionally, Damiana is widely used as an aphrodisiac and is known to naturally improve energy and physical drive.

Ingredients

- Two teaspoons of dried Damiana leaves
- 1 cup of boiling water
- Honey or lemon (optional, for taste)

Instructions

1. Place the dried Damiana leaves in a tea bag or straight into a cup.
2. Pour the hot water over the Damiana leaves.
3. Cover the cup and let it sit for 15-20 minutes. This long steeping time helps the active ingredients be fully cleared.
4. Remove the tea sieve or strain the tea to remove the leaves.
5. Add honey or a bit of lemon to taste, if desired.
6. Enjoy this beverage once or twice daily, especially in the evening, to take advantage of its relaxing and mood-enhancing benefits.

Variations

- For a more involved taste, add a cinnamon stick or a few slices of fresh ginger to the cup while steeping.
- Combine with peppermint leaves for a cool twist and extra stomach benefits.
- Mix Damiana with chamomile leaves during steeping to make a calming nighttime mix.

Storage Tips

Empty dried Damiana leaves should be stored in a covered jar in a cool, dark place to protect their usefulness. Prepared Damiana Leaf Infusion is best served fresh but can be kept in the refrigerator for up to 24 hours. Reheat gently before eating, or enjoy it cold.

Printed by Amazon Italia Logistica S.r.l.
Torrazza Piemonte (TO), Italy

64824032R00078